TikTok®

by Jesse Stay

TikTok® For Dummies®

Published by **John Wiley & Sons, Inc.**, 111 River Street, Hoboken, NJ 07030-5774, www.wiley.com

Copyright © 2021 by John Wiley & Sons, Inc., Hoboken, New Jersey

Published simultaneously in Canada

For general information on our other products and services, please contact our Customer Care Department within the U.S. at 877-762-2974, outside the U.S. at 317-572-3993, or fax 317-572-4002. For technical support, please visit https://hub.wiley.com/community/support/dummies.

Wiley publishes in a variety of print and electronic formats and by print-on-demand. Some material included with standard print versions of this book may not be included in e-books or in print-on-demand. If this book refers to media such as a CD or DVD that is not included in the version you purchased, you may download this material at http://booksupport.wiley.com. For more information about Wiley products, visit www.wiley.com.

Library of Congress Control Number: 2021936894

ISBN: 978-1-119-80341-6; ISBN (ePDF): 978-1-119-80342-3; ISBN (ePub): 978-1-119-80343-0

Manufactured in the United States of America

SKY10027323_052821

Table of Contents

Introduction

"Tick tock ya don't stop!" That quote was made famous by the popular boy band Color Me Badd. The well-known actor and talk show host Rosie O'Donnell uses the phrase in her TikTok videos. Once you're on TikTok, it's hard to stop!

There's a good chance you're here because your kids couldn't stop, and now you're on TikTok, too, wondering what the heck you're supposed to do next. I asked the same question when the daughters of a close friend (hi, Ellie and Reese) were on the app non-stop. As a writer of content about the future of technology, I was fascinated and wanted to discover what made TikTok "tick." In this book, I show you what I learned in the process.

About This Book

Each chapter in *TikTok For Dummies* operates on its own, and you don't have to read each chapter in order. As you swipe through the pages (some of you are reading this in electronic format and literally doing that!), you'll see that the book, like TikTok, is designed in bite-sized pieces.

You can sift through the pages randomly and still learn plenty — and, I hope, become amused and entertained in the process. Consider me your entertainer and the book your dopamine rush as you unravel the confusing world of this crazy new app you want to figure out.

Note that TikTok is constantly updating. As of this writing, rumors have flown around of three-minute videos becoming available. Some are trying to start false rumors about status updates similar to Facebook and Twitter. TikTok adds and removes effects and filters all the time. I did my best to include up-to-date information and keep it broadly written and as time indifferent as possible.

Foolish Assumptions

I'd rather not assume anything, but since there are so many of you, I have to assume a few things:

>> You have a mobile device (the desktop version is limited, so I focus on the mobile future of TikTok).

>> Your mobile device uses iOS or Android. My kids use their Amazon Kindle Fires, which operate on Android, so those devices work, too, with some limitations.

>> You can find, download, and access apps on your mobile phone.

>> You can perform the following basic phone gestures:

- *Tap:* Touch the screen lightly with one finger.

- *Swipe:* Quickly move a finger across the screen, left and right, or up and down.

- *Pinch/unpinch:* This gesture is often referred to as zooming in and out. Place two fingers on the screen and pull them apart to zoom in, making something onscreen larger and easier to see. Pull your two fingers together to zoom back out.

- *Long-press (or tap-and-hold):* Sometimes you need to do more than just tap to open a menu on TikTok. For instance, as a video plays, you can long-press it to display a menu. (I describe this menu in Chapter 2.)

- *Drag:* Tap-and-hold and then move your finger to another part of the screen. This is an important gesture when you're editing videos (see Chapter 3) and putting together a stitched video (see Chapter 9).

These are common actions needed to create videos and interact on TikTok. If you know these gestures, you can do anything in the app!

>> You're willing to think at least a little bit with your right brain and get fun and creative! I know, as an INTP on the Meyer's Briggs myself, that assumption is a hard one.

Icons Used in This Book

For your convenience, I've placed icons throughout the margins to help you understand more about the content I'm sharing.

TIP

I use the Tip icon to reveal helpful tidbits, some of which, I hope, will provide inspiration for your videos.

REMEMBER

When I want to jog your memory of something in the app or said elsewhere in the book, I use this icon to bring it back to mind.

WARNING

Pay attention to this stuff — don't skip it! Something might go wrong if you don't heed the advice here.

TECHNICAL STUFF

For the more geeky or those who like to learn, this info will take you to the next level or provide links where you can discover more.

Beyond the Book

This book comes with a cheat sheet that lists some of my favorite accounts to follow, beyond those mentioned in Chapter 12 and 13, tips and techniques for creating better videos, and ways I've used TikTok in my digital marketing business to earn income and grow audiences. To get to the cheat sheet, simply go to www.dummies.com and type *TikTok For Dummies Cheat Sheet* in the Search box.

I include links to my most relevant TikTok content on my Facebook page and Twitter account and also write updates on my blog when I can. (I can just hear the TikTok users saying, "Ew, Facebook!") Here are links to where you can find me on other platforms:

>> **My personal TikTok (to learn about and contact me):**
   https://tiktok.com/@jessestay

- **»** **This book's TikTok (to learn about TikTok and reference examples in the book):** https://tiktok.com/@tiktokfordummiesbook

- **»** **Facebook:** https://facebook.com/stay

- **»** **Twitter:** https://twitter.com/jesse

- **»** **LinkedIn:** https://linkedin.com/in/facebook

- **»** **My website/blog:** https://jessestay.com

- **»** **My email list:** https://jessestay.com/tiktokfordummies

Seriously — reach out any time and share with me what you're doing on TikTok. In addition to these channels, my email address is me@jessestay.com, and you can text me at +1-385-450-STAY. I'll do my best to answer as many of my readers as I can!

Following are other places I recommend you go to get started and for help beyond the links I've already shared include:

- **»** **This book's Facebook group (**https://facebook.com/groups/tiktokfordummies**):** Introduce yourself and see what you can learn from others and what you can do to help others!

- **»** **The article "A Beginner's Guide to TikTok" by Louise Matsakis, published by Wired (**www.wired.com/story/how-to-use-tik-tok**):** Although this article was published in 2019, it still has relevant information.

- **»** **The article "How to Create Your First TikTok Video" by Rachel Pedersen, published by Social Media Examiner (**www.socialmediaexaminer.com/how-to-create-your-first-tiktok-video**):** This is another super useful article with snazzy examples.

- **»** **Your kids or grandkids:** Some of my favorite TikTok accounts include kids featuring their famous parents. Mark Cuban's daughter (@alexis_cuban) has some hilarious ones. So does Chef Gordon Ramsay's daughter (@tillyramsay)! Incidentally, Cuban is my favorite *shark* from *Shark Tank,* as you'll learn from my TikTok account.

Where to Go from Here

If you need help signing in to TikTok and creating a profile, read Chapter 1. Then check out Chapter 2, where I describe all the ways to browse TikTok so you can find people you want to follow. Next, the best way to learn TikTok is to jump in and create videos. Chapters 3 and 4 provide details for creating and publishing your own videos.

I encourage you to discover as much as you can through this book and then by experimenting on TikTok. Check out Chapters 12 and 13 for some accounts I like to follow. Search for your favorite topics using the TikTok search function and the Discover page, which I introduce in Chapter 2 and describe more fully in Chapter 8, and then follow those new accounts.

When you're ready to take it to the next level, see Part 2, where you find out how to check your stats, and discover tips for creating content that will reach new audiences — and might just go viral. Part 3 is for those who want to use TikTok in their business.

Be goofy, learn from what others are doing, and have fun. Join some memes and trends. Dance like you've never danced. Lip sync like you've never lip synced. Follow as many people as you can, and you'll quickly get the hang of it. Tell your friends and family you're on TikTok and get them to follow you — they might even teach you a few things.

You've got this!

1

Getting Started with TikTok — the Movie Studio in Your Pocket

Sign up for TikTok and create your first video.

Learn how to surf TikTok and discover new content.

Record and upload videos.

Edit, apply effects to, and publish your video.

Study TikTok etiquette and culture.

Protect yourself and your family on TikTok.

Chapter **1**

Using TikTok for the First Time

Welcome to the amazing, different, and maybe even intimidating but addicting world of TikTok! There's a good chance your children or grandchildren sent you here, or you were swindled into trying out a TikTok dance, prank, or meme from a friend or loved one. Whatever the reason, the question I keep hearing is, "How do I use this crazy app?"

Well, I'm here, as your furry, lovable (repeating Grover from *Sesame Street*) TikTok creator, to show you how. I teach you the way I know best and am most comfortable with: by writing a book. (As you soon discover, younger TikTok users would wonder why I'm not creating TikTok videos instead.)

Downloading TikTok for Your Mobile Device

Downloading TikTok is the easiest part. TikTok works on both Android and iOS. I even got it to work on my children's Kindle Fire devices, which are Android-based. Because you already have one of these (see my foolish assumptions in the Introduction), search for the Google Play app (Android) or the App Store (iOS). After you are in either of these app stores, do the following:

1. **Find the search functionality in Google Play or the App Store.**

   A big Search icon usually appears at the bottom or top of the screen. On my iPhone, the Search icon is in the bottom right.

2. **Search for *TikTok*, as shown in Figure 1-1.**

3. **Tap the download icon (iPhone) or the Install button (Android).**

   The the download icon is a down arrow or a cloud if you've previously downloaded the app (as in Figure 1-1). It may look slightly different on your device.

That's it. Now I show you how to create an account so you can start using the app.

FIGURE 1-1:
Searching and downloading the TikTok app.

TIP

On Kindle Fire devices, the TikTok app is in the Kindle app store. However, keep in mind that your app experience may be limited on Kindle Fire in terms of camera quality and the speed of the app.

Creating Your Account

After you've downloaded the TikTok app to your mobile device, the first step in using the service is to create an account. When you open the app, you're greeted with a Sign Up for TikTok screen, as shown in Figure 1-2.

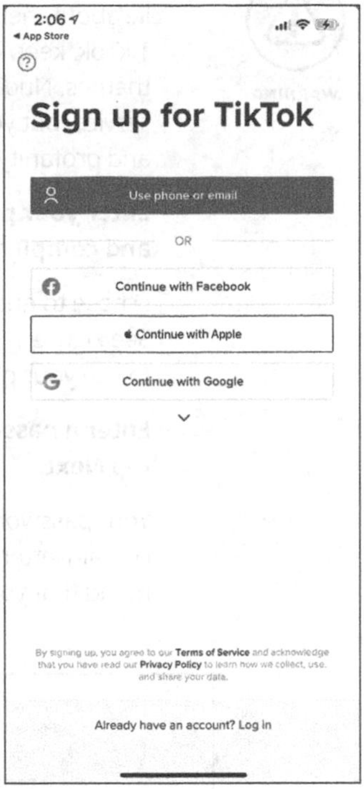

You can sign up with your phone number, your email address, or your Facebook, Apple (if on iOS), Google, or Twitter account. (Twitter is available by tapping the down arrow below the Continue with Google option.) Signing up with an account is the easiest option because Tik-Tok autofills many of the sections.

Follow these steps to create your TikTok account:

FIGURE 1-2:
The account setup process.

1. **Tap one of the following:**

   - *Use Phone or Email button:* I recommend this option so you can understand the full registration process. Then continue with Step 2.

   - *The button representing your Internet account of choice.* If you insist on taking the shorter route (hey — I don't blame you!) by tapping the Continue with Facebook, Continue with Apple, Continue with Google, or Continue with Twitter button (to see the Twitter option, tap the down arrow), just follow the on-screen instructions to log into your chosen account. After you're authenticated, skip to Step 5, where you're asked to choose a username.

2. **Enter your birthday and then tap Next.**

You must be 13 or older to use TikTok. While some parents lie about their children's ages so that their kids can use TikTok, keep in mind that many videos on TikTok have adult themes. Nudity and illegal activities are not allowed on the service, but your children will be exposed to adult topics and profanity if they use the app.

3. **Enter your phone number or email address, tap Next, and complete the Captcha puzzle.**

I chose to enter an email, which is selected by default. See Figure 1-3, left. Tap Email in the upper right if you prefer to use your phone number.

4. **Enter a password, as shown in Figure 1-3, right, and then tap Next.**

Your password must be 8 to 20 characters long, and must contain letters, numbers, and special characters. I recommend that you use a password manager such as LastPass.

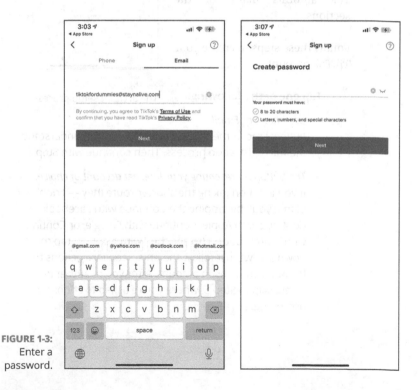

FIGURE 1-3: Enter a password.

5. **Pick a unique username for your account.**

Your username is how your account will be identified publicly. If the username is taken, you see a message saying, *This username isn't available*. Don't worry — you can change your username later if you're not entirely sure which username to choose right now!

6. **Choose your interests — or not. Then tap Next.**

If you want, select what you want to see most on TikTok. If you'd rather not fill out this part, click the Skip link.

Congratulations! You have a TikTok account. The app will play a little video showing you how to use TikTok, and take you to the For You page, shown in Figure 1-4.

FIGURE 1-4:
The For You page.

TIP

After you create an account and watch the introductory tutorials, the TikTok app will ask you to allow notifications on your phone, as shown in Figure 1-5 (if you haven't previously enabled notifications). I suggest that you turn on notifications for now so you can become familiar with the app and have the app top of mind as you learn how to use it. You can always turn off notifications later in your device's Settings screen.

FIGURE 1-5:
TikTok wants you to turn on notifications.

TikTok, like all apps and social networks, is constantly making changes to its interface, and some options may be slightly different than they are here. Please feel free to ask questions in the Facebook Group I set up for this book at https://facebook.com/groups/tiktokfordummies.

The For You page (refer to Figure 1-4) is the default view for TikTok when you open the app. It's where you can discover new content and users to follow. The other view, Following, displays content from those you are already following. You can switch from one to the other by tapping For You or Following at the top of the page or by swiping right or left.

On either page, swipe up as often as you like for an endless dopamine rush of new content to explore! I discuss the For You and Following pages, and how to discover and follow new content, in Chapter 2.

Exploring Your Settings

People go to your profile page when they want to learn more about you. After you create your account and have had a chance to get acclimated, I recommend that you edit your profile to give the best picture of yourself to the outside world. You might want to update your profile picture (called your *avatar*), username, and description, along with other information. You might also want to change some settings so they are more to your liking.

If you're really excited about creating a video right now, you can skip this section and go to the "Creating Your First TikTok Video" section, later in the chapter. You can always change your profile and user settings later. However, editing your settings now (by adding a photo and bio) will ensure that others know who you are and give them a reason to follow you, which will help you get more views from the start!

Updating your profile

You can get to your profile from any main TikTok page by clicking the Me icon (the little person) in the lower right. Then to edit your profile, tap Edit Profile. The page shown in Figure 1-6 appears.

You change the following options on this page:

>> **Change Photo:** Tap Change Photo and then tap either Take Photo or Upload Photo (or Select from Gallery on Android). If you want to take a photo with your device camera, select Take Photo and then take a selfie. Otherwise, tap Upload Photo or Select from Gallery and select a photo from your device's photo library. (You can view the photo after you take or upload it.)

3:48	
	Edit profile
Change photo	Change video
Name	TikTok For Dummies >
Username	tiktokfordummiesbook >
	tiktok.com/@tiktokfordummiesbook
Bio	Jesse Stay's (@jessestay) official acco... >
Nonprofit	Add nonprofit to your profile >
Instagram	Add Instagram to your profile >
YouTube	Add YouTube to your profile >

FIGURE 1-6:
The Edit Profile page on my first visit.

The profile photo you choose appears next to every comment you make, so be sure your photo represents the way you want to be seen.

When you add a photo, TikTok also lets you add a video to your profile. Only those who visit your profile and click the video can see it.

>> **Name:** If you signed up using another social media platform, your name on that platform appears here. If you signed up using your phone number or email, TikTok generates a name, such as user1234567. This name appears at the top of your profile when other viewers visit your profile page, so be sure it's descriptive of you or your brand! If you want to change the Name field, tap Name, make your changes, and then tap Save.

REMEMBER

TIP

>> **Username:** You added a unique username when you created your account. To change it, tap Username, enter another unique username, and then tap Save. (Remember, a green check mark appears if the username hasn't been chosen by anyone else.)

You can change your username only once every 30 days. Also, it's unclear when or if TikTok releases old usernames, so choose carefully because you may not be able to reuse an old username.

>> **Bio:** Tap Bio and add a brief (80 characters or less) description about yourself. Your bio should grab people's attention and give them a reason to follow you. Be witty or funny if you like. Then tap Save in the upper right to return to the Edit Profile page.

>> **Nonprofit:** This option is new. If you want to choose a nonprofit you love, TikTok will display it prominently on your profile and give your followers an option to donate. I think the Nonprofit option will evolve over time.

>> **Instagram:** You can feature a single Instagram account on your profile by tapping Instagram and following the instructions in the Instagram authentication process.

>> **YouTube:** You can include on your profile a link to one of your YouTube channels. To feature a YouTube channel, tap the YouTube option, and then follow the instructions to authenticate your Google account and choose your YouTube account.

When all your info is filled out, your account should look similar to Figure 1-7. (I didn't add a YouTube or Instagram account to my profile page.)

FIGURE 1-7:
My simple profile page.

Your profile looks nice and pretty now! In the next section you learn how to make your TikTok experience safer by editing your profile settings and privacy features.

Updating your profile and privacy settings

Now that you've edited your profile to your liking, you should become familiar with the Settings and Privacy page. This is where you discover how to protect yourself, set the level of privacy you're comfortable with, and even gain access to your profile statistics. To start, tap the three dots icon in the upper right of your profile page (refer to Figure 1-7). The Settings and Privacy page appears, as shown in Figure 1-8.

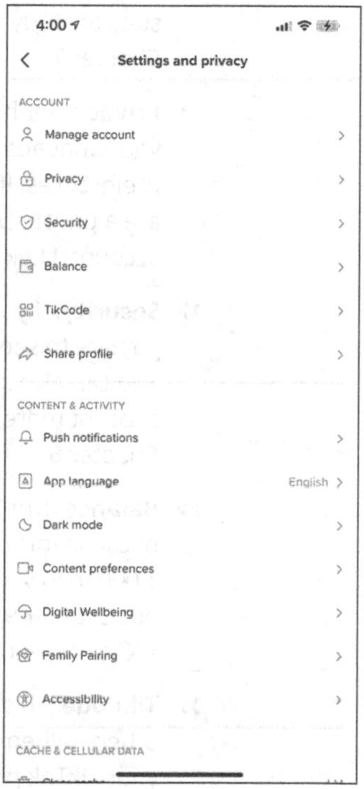

REMEMBER

For space constraints, I list the most important options here (and describe some of them in more detail in Chapters 6 and 9). Many of the following options will change over time because TikTok regularly updates its design and functionality. If any of these options don't exist or look different, feel free to ask a question in the Facebook Group I set up for readers. You can join at `https://facebook.com/ groups/tiktokfordummies`.

FIGURE 1-8:
The Settings and Privacy page.

Following are the major options available:

- » **Manage Account:** If necessary, add a phone number, add an email address, or update your password to log into your account.

  You can also delete your account here if you want to start over (and start this chapter from the beginning). You can also switch to a free Pro Account, which enables you to get stats to study your account followers and video views (see Chapter 7).

- » **Privacy:** Set how public your account is, how people find you, what ads know about you, and communication preferences. If you're creating an account for your kids or are a private person, you can set the account as a private account. I talk more about privacy settings in Chapter 6.

- » **Security:** If you get an alert indicating suspicious activity, go here to see which devices are logging into your account. You can also set up two-step verification to make your account more secure. I describe security in more detail in Chapter 6.

- » **Balance:** Don't worry about the Balance setting right now because this option applies only when you have more than 1,000 followers. In case you do hit 1,000 followers, check out Chapter 9, where I talk about the Balance option and TikTok revenue-sharing features for livestreams.

- » **TikCode:** This option gives you a QR code to share with others. When people scan the code, they link directly to your TikTok profile.

TIP

Do this right now: Tap TikCode, tap Save to Device, and then share the image (it's usually in your device's Photos app) on your other social networks so others can follow you. People can also scan the QR code image on their phones to automatically load your TikTok profile and begin following your TikTok videos.

Figure 1-9 is the TikCode for the TikTok profile I set up for this book. Try scanning the QR code in the figure by tapping TikCode under Settings and Privacy in your TikTok app, and then tapping the Scan icon at the bottom. This loads the book's TikTok profile. Then tap Follow to follow my updates for this book on TikTok!

A QR code is a square bar code that most modern phones can read. It usually represents a hyperlink to a website.

>> **Share Profile:** The Share Profile setting, like the TikCode setting, is a way to share your profile with others. Tapping the Share Profile setting takes you to your mobile device's default Share screen.

The Settings and Privacy page has dozens of other options. For now, the ones I mention here are sufficient to get you started and keep you safe.

FIGURE 1-9:
The TikCode for the TikTok account created for the book.

Now it's time to have fun. In the next section, I teach you some basic elements of the TikTok interface while you create your first video!

Creating Your First TikTok Video

Creating TikTok videos is easy. Maybe you already created a video when TikTok prompted you to try after you set up your account. I dive deeper into video creation and all its features in Chapter 3. Here, I describe the basic elements:

1. **Tap the plus (+) icon.**

   The plus icon appears at the bottom of the screen after you log in (refer to Figure 1-7).

If this is your first time using the app or opening the recording screen, give the app permission to access your camera, audio, and photo library.

2. **Look over the recording page, which is shown in Figure 1-10.**

The recording page is the "movie studio in your pocket" that I reference throughout the book. For now, become familiar with the following elements:

- The big red record button near the bottom
- The Effects icon, to the left of the red record button
- The 60s and 15s video length options at the bottom of the screen

FIGURE 1-10: The recording page has everything you need to create content!

I describe the other elements on this screen in Chapter 3.

3. **Select your video length.**

Tap 60s for anything greater than 15 seconds (to a maximum of 60 seconds), or leave this option at the default 15s for videos up to 15 seconds.

4. **(Optional) Choose an effect.**

Effects are optional, but I wanted to include a description to show you how fun TikTok can be:

a. *Tap Effects to the left of the red record button and browse through the effects, as shown in Figure 1-11.* TikTok, similar to apps such as Snapchat, usually provides instructions on how to use the effect.

b. *Tap an effect you like and try it out by following the instructions on the screen.* Select another effect if you don't like that one. Feel free to scroll through and try them all.

c. *Tap anywhere outside the Effects dialog to return to the recording screen.* Or tap the circle with a line in the upper left of the Effects dialog if you decide you don't want to use any effects. The effect begins when you start recording, as shown in Step 6.

FIGURE 1-11:
Scroll through the many effects available on TikTok.

5. **Place what you want to record inside the frame.**

Choose what you want to record, and place that person or thing inside the camera frame. Note that you can tap the Flip icon or double-tap anywhere on the screen to flip the camera view.

6. **Tap the red record button.**

If you tap the button once, TikTok will record automatically until you either tap the button briefly again or your 15-second or 60-second time is up. You can also long-press (press and hold down) the record button, and the TikTok app will record for as long as you hold down that button or your time is up.

TIP

Long-pressing the record button can be useful for — wait for it (you're about to be smarter than 80 percent of TikTok users) — zooming! To try it, long-press the record button and, with your finger still down, slide the button up to zoom in and down to zoom out. Boom! Instant zoom as you're recording. When you release the button, TikTok stops recording.

7. **If you finish filming before reaching the time limit (15 or 60 seconds) click the red check mark in the bottom-right corner.**

When you finish recording your video, the page shown in Figure 1-12 appears — either automatically or after you tap the check mark. (The figure shows me typing this very section of Chapter 1 — how meta!)

8. **(Optional) Add sounds or additional effects. Then tap Next.**

You can choose sounds and other effects to add to your video, which I cover in Chapter 3.

9. **Add a description and configure sharing options.**

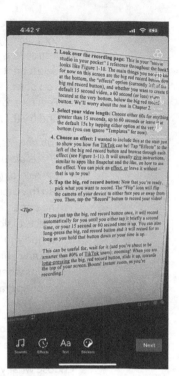

FIGURE 1-12: Editing your just recorded video.

On the next page, shown in Figure 1-13, add a description about your video (150 characters or less). I usually tap the #Hashtags button and select a popular hashtag or two to add to the video. (If you used an effect in your video, TikTok may automatically add a hashtag for that effect in the description; you can keep it or delete it.)

I also suggest turning on the Allow Duet and Allow Stitch options to allow others to share your video. Just tap each slider and it will move to the on position and turn green. I explain Allow Duet, Allow Stitch, and the other options you see here in Chapters 3 and 9.

10. **To post your video, tap the Post button.**

If this is your first time posting a video, you're asked to verify that it's okay to publish the video publicly. If you want your creation to be seen by the world, tap Post Now. If you would rather it remain private, skip to Chapter 6, where I cover privacy for your profile and your videos, or simply select Me Only under Who Can Watch This Video.

The For You page appears, with the video you just created uploading in the upper-left corner, along with videos from other recommended video creators, which TikTok selects for you, if you're not following anyone yet.

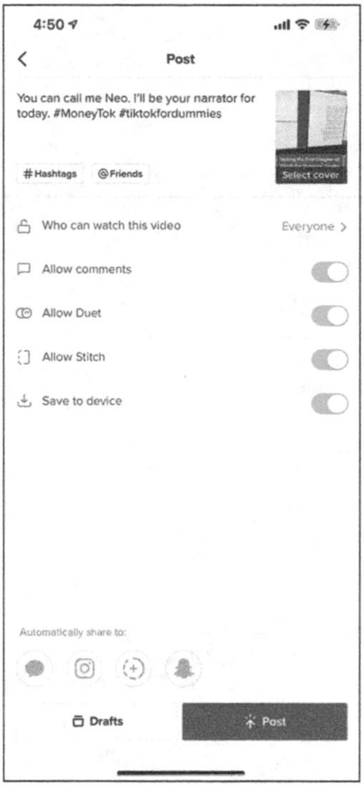

FIGURE 1-13:
Your final recording page.

When the video has finished uploading, it will play automatically on the For You or Following page as long as you keep the app open, repeating itself over and over unless you tap the screen to pause. Congratulations! You just created your first TikTok video.

In the next chapter, you discover how to find and follow content on TikTok. Then in Chapter 3, you get to know the other recording elements and fully use the "movie studio in your pocket" that is TikTok video creation.

Chapter **2**

Browsing TikTok

reating videos is what makes TikTok "tick," but TikTok wouldn't be what it is without the ability for users to discover, interact with, and share videos. The beauty of TikTok is that it gives you not only a "movie studio in your pocket" but also the resources and platform to reach potentially millions of people.

TikTok has an amazing, thriving community, consisting of users in just about any niche imaginable! You can almost guarantee one of your favorite things to talk about or share, in video format, has an interested, captive audience already waiting to see your content. In this chapter, you discover how to begin interacting with and watching content by this amazing community.

Browsing on the Home Screen

One of the first things you see when you download and create an account on TikTok is the For You page (FYP) on your Home screen. The For You page is a collection of videos that TikTok thinks you'll enjoy based on the videos you like and view in the app. (You see a random selection of videos the first time you visit the For You page.)

Next to the For You page at the top of the Home screen is the Following page, displaying videos posted by TikTok users you follow. Your Following page is accessible as soon as you start following other users. I show you how to do that later in this chapter.

To access the For You or Following page, tap Home in the bottom-left corner of the screen. If the last page you visited before venturing elsewhere in the app was the For You page (see Figure 2-1), you're taken to the For You page after tapping Home (and For You is highlighted in brighter white). If the last page you visited was the Following page, you're taken to the Following page. Either way, a video will be playing on repeat, with icons for engaging on the right side of the screen. I discuss those icons later in the chapter.

If you can't see the Home icon, tap the left-pointing arrow in the upper left of your screen until you get back to where you can see the main navigation options at the bottom of the screen.

Courtesy of Mikayla Brianne (@_mikaylabrianne)

FIGURE 2-1:
The For You page.

> To switch between the Following page and the For You page, tap For You (or Following) at the top or swipe left or right.

Here are ways you can navigate videos on both the For You and Following pages:

> » **To go to the next video, swipe up.** A new, never-before-seen video plays on repeat.

>> **To go back to the previous video, swipe down.** The last video you watched (before swiping up) plays.

>> **To pause (and resume) the currently playing video, tap anywhere on your screen.** The video pauses. To resume, tap anywhere on the screen again.

Liking and Commenting

As you navigate through videos on the Home screen, you can interact and do things with each video you watch. You can tap any of the four icons on the right of the Home screen as videos play:

>> **Video creator's profile pic:** Tap this icon to see the user's public profile. If you don't follow this person, a plus sign appears next to their profile pic. You can see how many people the person is following, how many people follow that person, and more. Tap < (upper left) to go back to the video.

TIP

The profile picture is small, and if you haven't followed the user, you might accidentally tap the plus sign instead, following the user when you didn't intend to. Another way to view the user's profile page is to tap the username in the bottom left of the screen.

>> **Heart:** Tap this icon once to like the video. Tap it again to unlike the video. You can also double-tap a video to like it.

>> **Comment (word balloon):** One of the first things you might feel prompted to do is comment on the video, as you would on many other social networks. See the following steps for details on commenting.

>> **Share (right-pointing arrow or three dots):** Tap the arrow (or the three dots if you've previously shared this video) to see the Send To menu. You can save the video, share it via other apps such as Messenger and Twitter, send it to friends, and perform more advanced sharing actions such as duetting and stitching, which I discuss in Chapter 8. I discuss the Send To menu in the next section, "Sharing Videos."

For a fun effect that does nothing but like the video, tap the screen more than once. Multiple hearts appear, expanding and disappearing, as shown in Figure 2-2. (The more you tap, the more hearts appear.)

As you scroll through your For You or Following pages, you might want to say something to the video creator. To comment on a video:

1. **Tap the comment icon (word balloon).**

The comment screen pops up, showing all the comments currently on the video and a box at the bottom to add your own, as shown in Figure 2-3.

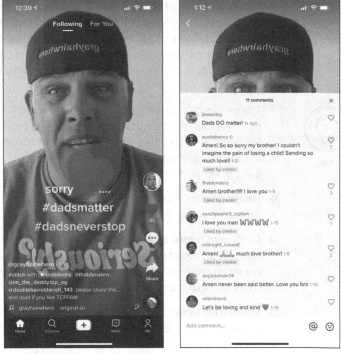

Courtesy of Marcel Roston (@grayhairwhere)

FIGURE 2-2:
Add animated hearts if you really like the video.

Courtesy of Marcel Roston (@grayhairwhere)

FIGURE 2-3:
A list of comments.

2. **Tap the Add Comment box and start typing with the keyboard that appears.**

3. **To mention other users, tap the @ icon and type the person's username.**

4. **To add an emoji to your comment, tap the smiley face icon and select an emoji, or select from the list of popular emojis shown above the keyboard.**

5. **When your comment is complete, tap Send.**

   The keyboard disappears, revealing the list of comments again, with your comment at the top.

6. **To like a comment, tap its heart icon.**

   The heart turns red. To unlike, tap the heart again.

Your comment is now posted on the video and you're officially a comment aficionado! To get back to the video, tap anywhere outside the comment screen.

Liking and commenting are the most familiar ways to engage and interact with videos. But did you know that there's a secret list of options to interact with videos? Here's how you unlock the secret: On any video on your Home page, press down on the video, and a menu appears with these options (see Figure 2-4):

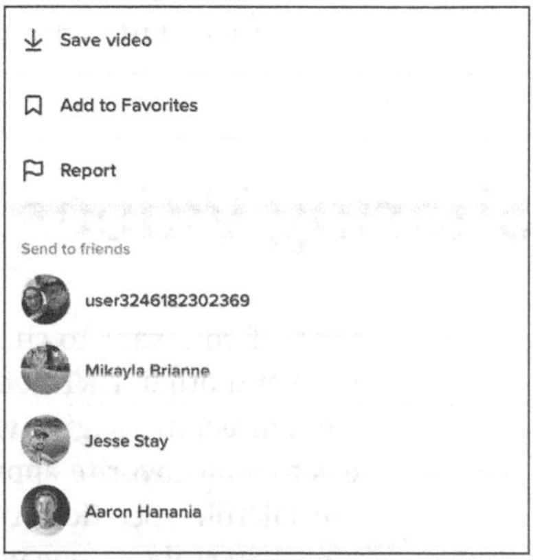

↓ Save video

🔖 Add to Favorites

🏳 Report

Send to friends

(•) user3246182302369

(•) Mikayla Brianne

(•) Jesse Stay

(•) Aaron Hanania

FIGURE 2-4: The secret video actions menu.

» **Save Video:** Save the video to your device's default photo storage. A Share To menu appears, giving you the option to share to other apps installed on your device. To go back to the video, tap Done or tap anywhere outside the menu.

>> **Add to Favorites:** Add the video to your favorite videos (only visible by you) on your profile page. You then return to the video.

>> **Report:** Report a video as inappropriate by selecting a reason from the list that appears. See Chapter 6 for details. Depending what you choose, you might see another list to refine your reason, until finally you can tap Submit. Tap X (upper right) or < (upper left) to return to the video without reporting it.

>> **Send to Friends:** Send the video to someone you follow. Tap More Friends to see a longer list and to display a Search box. To search for someone, type in the Search box at top. Tap X (in the upper right) if you change your mind. After you tap a name, you return to the video, and it appears in your friend's inbox.

TIP

You can also tap the Not Interested icon if you don't want to see videos similar to the one you're currently watching. Tapping More on the Not Interested tab enables you to choose to hide videos from that user or videos using the sound of the video you're watching.

Sharing Videos

What if you want to share videos you really like with your audience and other TikTok users? You have multiple ways to do this, from direct messaging videos to people you follow to sharing videos to your favorite apps and duetting or stitching. (The last two are TikTok-specific actions that allow you to interact and share videos in truly unique ways. See Chapter 8 for more.)

To share any video in the For You or Following pages, tap the share icon (right-pointing arrow). The send menu appears, as shown in Figure 2-5.

The following options are available:

>> **Send To:** At the top is a list of TikTok users you follow.

1. *Tap a circle to send the video to that user.* You can tap more than one, and a check mark appears on each circle. A box to send a message appears below it.

2. *To select from a larger list of TikTok users you follow, tap More at the far right of the user list.*

3. *To type a message with the video, tap in the Send a Message box and type using the keyboard that appears.*

FIGURE 2-5:
The Send To menu.

4. *When you're ready, tap Send* (see Figure 2-6). The video you're sharing is sent as a DM to the users you selected, and you return to the video on your Home screen.

FIGURE 2-6:
Sending users a message with a selected video.

» **Share To:** You see a list of apps on your device that you can share the video with. Sharing outside TikTok is easy. In Figure 2-7, I tapped the Facebook icon and a screen appeared prompting me to add text to a new Facebook post, with the video embedded below. Each app has different options, so refer to each app's documentation to learn how to share.

You can tap the Copy Link button at the bottom of the app list to copy to the clipboard a link to the video. You can then paste the link elsewhere. When someone clicks the link, the video will open in a web browser.

FIGURE 2-7:
Sharing a TikTok video to Facebook.

» **Additional options:** At the bottom of the screen you see more options:

- *Report, Save Video, Add to Favorites:* These options work the same as when you access them through the secret video actions menu (refer to Figure 2-4), which I describe earlier in the chapter.

  If you're on the For You page, you can also tap the Not Interested icon if you don't want to see similar videos.

- *Duet:* You can add your recording to another creator's video. I discuss duetting in Chapter 8.

- *Stitch:* You can use up to five seconds of another creator's video in your own recording. See Chapter 8.

- *Live Photo:* Save your video as a live photo if you're on iOS. The video doesn't include sound.

- *GIF:* Share the video as an animated graphic. The video doesn't include sound.

- *Use This Effect:* Begin a new recording, automatically applying the effect listed in the video you're watching.

Listening to Your Audience: Direct Messages and Inbox Notifications

After you create a video or two of your own on TikTok, other users will start following your account after seeing the video on the For You page. As this happens, those users might want to like, comment on, duet, or stitch your videos. But how do you know they're interacting with your videos? You can find all your own followers' interactions in your inbox.

Let me take you on a tour. To get acclimated to your inbox, start by tapping the Inbox icon at the bottom of the screen. If you don't see the typical navigation options with a + in the middle, tap the back arrow (<) in the upper left until you see these navigation options at the bottom.

Your inbox page appears (as shown in Figure 2-8, left), featuring the following items:

>> **All Activity drop-down menu:** At the top is a menu for selecting the types of activity you want to see: All Activity (the default view), Likes, Comments, Q&A, Mentions, Followers, and From TikTok. (See Figure 2-8, right.)

Q&A is a new feature that enables anyone visiting your profile to ask you questions, which you can answer by creating a new video. You can turn on the feature in Settings and Privacy, which you can access from your profile page. When enabled, a Q&A button appears on your profile page for viewers to tap.

>> **Direct Messages (DMs) icon:** Tap this icon to see your direct messages. The icon has a red, circled number on it when you have new DMs.

>> **Activity feed:** The main part of the screen is where you'll see all activity on all your videos and any new users who have followed you. The list is sorted by date (with the newest activity first).

Following are the types of activity you'll see in your activity feed and how to identify them:

>> **User comments on others' videos mentioning your username:** A comment from another user on TikTok that mentions you (by typing @ followed by your username) starts with "*(username)* mentioned you in a comment:" in the activity feed.

>> **User comments on your videos:** A comment on one of your own videos starts with "*(username)* commented:" in the activity feed. Replies to comments you have made appear as "*(username)* replied to your comment."

>> **Duets and stitches of videos you created and mentions of your username elsewhere on TikTok:** If someone duetted, stitched, or just mentioned you in the description of his or her video or in the comments elsewhere on TikTok, your activity feed shows an item that starts with, "*(username)* mentioned you in a video."

>> **Likes of your videos:** If someone likes your video, the activity feed shows a line that starts with *"(username) liked* your video."

>> **People following your account:** If someone follows you on TikTok, the activity feed shows a line that starts with *"(username)* started following you."

Responding to comments and mentions

In your inbox notifications, when you see a comment or a mention of your username inside another comment on TikTok, you may want to reply to that comment. To see just the comments (or mentions) in your inbox notifications, tap the All Activity dropdown and select Comments (or Mentions).

To reply to a comment or mention, follow these steps:

1. **Tap the line of the inbox notifications with the comment or mention you want to reply to.**

   You're taken to the corresponding comments menu, with the selected comment at the top, as shown in Figure 2-9.

   TIP

   If you're responding to a mention in another video's description (such as someone stitching or duetting one of your own videos, or a mention with the @ symbol to get your attention), the

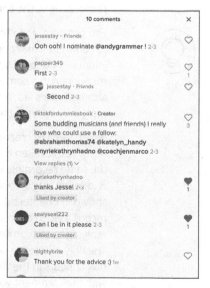

FIGURE 2-9:
The comment you selected from the Inbox notifications is at the top.

video you're tagged in appears. Tap the comments icon for that video and type a response to the video in the comments — or do another duet or stitch of your own if you want to respond that way!

2. **Tap the selected comment.**

A keyboard appears, prompting you to type your reply. If the comment is on one of the videos you created, a red camera icon appears to the left of the comment, as shown in Figure 2-10.

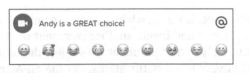

3. **Type your comment or record a video of yourself responding to the comment.**

TIP

You can do a video reply only to comments that appear on your own videos. If you're mentioned in a comment on another user's video, you can reply only by typing text.

If you opted to create a video reply, you're taken through the same recording, editing, and publishing screens shown in Chapters 3 and 4 to record a video of yourself replying to the comment. The only difference is that a box appears in the video, with the comment you're responding to for your viewers to see, as shown in Figure 2-11.

FIGURE 2-11:
A video reply, with the text of the comment it's responding to shown in the video.

4. **Tap Send (for text) or Publish (for a video).**

If you typed text, you return to the comments menu and your text reply appears nested below the comment you replied to.

If you recorded a video reply, your new video is nested below the comment you're replying to (the description of your video reply appears as the text of your reply, with a link to see the video). The video appears also on your profile page as a new video, which shows up in your followers' following pages.

You've got mail! Checking your DMs

TikTok allows users to send private messages to each other, via direct messages (DMs). You can access these through your inbox. To respond to a direct message and start a new conversation:

1. **In your inbox, tap the DM icon (paper airplane).**

The direct messages screen appears, with a list of your DMs on one screen.

2. **Tap any message you want to read.**

A conversation screen with that individual appears.

3. **Type your message in the Send a Message box (at the bottom) and then tap Send.**

Your message appears in the conversation, on the right of the screen below the last message of your private conversation.

4. **To start a new conversation:**

a. *Tap < in the upper left to return to the direct messages screen.*

b. *Tap the + sign in the upper right.* A list of users to send to appears below the Search box.

c. *Select from the list of users or type a user's name in the Search box.* A private conversation screen appears.

d. *Repeat Step 3 to write a new direct message to your selected user.*

Discovering Users and Content

As you scroll through TikTok, you'll probably come across interesting content that makes you think, "Hmm. I want to see more from that user!" You may have already followed a person or two and are craving more content from interesting users. You have several ways to find users who consistently produce amazing and entertaining content:

>> **The For You page:** This page is the most common way to discover new people to follow. Swipe up repeatedly on your For You page and you'll soon be addicted, seeing videos you want to see more of, and following their creators to get more of that content. TikTok can be a source of entertainment, but it can also be your place to get news, learn new topics, and discover that you're not alone with communities of people similar to yourself!

>> **The Discover page:** Tap Discover in the bottom navigation menu to see a page constantly updated by TikTok, curated with top trends, hashtags, trending sounds and music, and more! Or use the Search field at the top to search for music, hashtags, usernames, or videos that interest you.

>> **Your community of followers:** Another way to discover new content and users to follow is by interacting with, commenting on, duetting with, and stitching videos from users in your own community. As you interact with your community in your comments and elsewhere, users who discover your content on their own For You page will do the same, and you may come across new people in the areas and topics that interest you. Take advantage of those opportunities to interact and look over the content of followers who interact with your videos to see if you might want to follow them back.

TIP

Following every user who follows you is a controversial topic in the social media world. I know, because I, your ever-so-humble author, created the first tool for social media that did this automatically for people. (The tool no longer exists.) Following every person back who follows you can build trust and friendship with your followers. At the same time, it clutters your Following page, making it harder for you to discover great content and have better interactions with followers you're truly interested in.

Following a user on TikTok is easy. You have two ways to do it:

» On any video on the For You page, tap the + sign on the person's profile picture on the right. The + sign disappears, and you're now following that user's content, which appears in your Following page.

» Tap the Follow button on any user's profile page. (From the For You page, tap the person's profile picture once; from anywhere on TikTok, tap the person's username.) The Follow button is replaced with the friendship icon, showing that you follow each other (see Figure 2-12). If you follow the person but the person doesn't follow you, the icon has a check mark.

Courtesy of Mikayla Brianne (@_mikaylabrianne)

FIGURE 2-12:
A friendship icon appears next to the Message button.

Chapter **3**

Diving Deeper: Creating TikTok Videos

I n Chapter 1, I show you the basics of making your first TikTok video. If you've read Chapter 1 or 2 already, you're probably excited to dive deeper at this point, and maybe even start homing in on that overly creative right brain of yours.

But even if you feel that your creative side is minimal or non-existent, no problem: TikTok provides all the tools you need to create videos, add effects and filters, and post professional-looking videos as though you're a real-life movie director. TikTok will quickly become your "movie studio in your pocket." And who knows — maybe you'll even become TikTok famous for one of your video creations! In this chapter, you find everything you need to know to start creating and editing videos.

Starting a Recording

TikTok's entire user experience is built around creating videos that others can watch, like, share, and interact with in various ways. It should be no surprise, then, that TikTok makes recording videos easy: Just tap the big + icon (see Figure 3-1), which appears almost anywhere you are in the interface.

To begin recording:

1. **Tap the + icon, which is in the bottom-center of most screens in TikTok.**

   The recording screen appears, as shown in Figure 3-2.

   TIP

   If you don't see the + icon, just tap the < icon in the upper left of your screen until you see the + icon again, or close and reopen the TikTok app.

FIGURE 3-1:
The + icon for creating videos is at the bottom of the screen.

FIGURE 3-2:
The recording screen.

2. **Select a video length.**

The two options are 15s (up to 15 seconds, the default) and 60s (up to 60s seconds). I recommend starting with the default and moving to longer videos as you become more comfortable. (I describe the Templates option, next to 15s, at the end of the chapter.)

3. **(Optional) Tap the Flip icon to choose your device's front-facing or rear-facing camera, as shown in Figure 3-2.**

The Flip icon is in the top-right corner of the recording screen. If you see yourself on the recording screen and tap the Flip icon, the screen displays what's facing away from you, and vice versa.

You can also double-tap anywhere on the recording screen to flip the camera.

4. **(Optional) Tap the Speed icon (below the Flip icon) and then tap the speed of your recording.**

The Speed options appear in Figure 3-3. The numbers listed are in recording time. The 0.3x option records your video really fast (it's sped up 3 times) but plays it back more slowly. If you record in this speed, you'll sound like a chipmunk. The 3x option achieves the opposite: Your video will record more slowly than it plays back. Recording in 3x, you'll sound like you have a really low voice!

FIGURE 3-3:
The speed options.

5. **(Optional) Choose effects, settings, and filters for your video.**

Later in this chapter, I describe how to use the Beauty, Filters, Flash (Android), and Timer icons, as well as the effects accessed by tapping the Effects icon, which is next to the record button.

6. **Start recording your video using one of the following methods:**

- *Quick-tap method:* Simply tap the record button, and your video begins. It stops automatically after 15 seconds (or 60, if that's the length you chose).

- *Tap-and-hold method:* Press down on the record button to record.

TIP

A few seconds after you start recording using either method, a check mark appears next to the record button (see Figure 3-4). If using the quick-tap method, tap the check mark (rather than tapping record a second time) if you want to stop recording and go straight to the editing screen. If using the tap-and-hold method, release the record button and tap the check mark to go to the editing screen. If you use up the entire length of video, TikTok takes you automatically to the editing screen, no matter which method you use.

FIGURE 3-4:
The check mark appears after a few seconds of recording.

7. **(Optional) Pause and then continue recording using one of the following methods:**

- *Quick-tap method:* Tap the stop button to pause, and then tap the record button to continue recording.

- *Tap-and-hold method:* Remove your finger to pause, and press down on the record button again to continue recording.

While paused, you can add some (but not all) effects and filters and other fun things to the video. More about editing this way in Chapter 4.

8. **To stop recording:**

- *Quick-tap method:* Tap the stop button.

- *Tap-and-hold method:* Lift your finger from the record button.

    The app stops recording, but you remain on the recording screen.

You can repeat Steps 3–8, and flip the camera, add effects and filters, and change the speed (by pausing and starting to record again) as often as you like until your recording reaches the speci-fied video length, at which point the recording stops. Or to delete your previous recording, tap the backspace icon (with an x) to the right of the record button, as shown in Figure 3-5.

See Chapter 4 for details about editing after you've stopped recording and posting your video for the world to see.

The previous steps take you through a bare-bones process to record a video. As you continue making videos, you'll want to be more adventurous and incorporate the following actions — as well as sounds, music, and other effects! — into your videos:

>> **Zooming:** You can zoom during your recording using the quick-tap method by pinching and spreading two fingers on the screen. This method isn't as easy to do as when you use the tap-and-hold method to record.

TIP

If you're using the tap-and-hold method, slide your finger up or down to zoom in or out, respectively, while holding down the record button. Many TikTok users film themselves in a bathroom mirror (where there's good lighting), and zoom in as they record for added effect. In the quick-tap method, pinch and spread two figures on the screen.

>> **Using a tripod:** Set your device on a tripod and tap the record button — now your hands are free while recording. With the quick-tap method, you're untethered from your device and free. (Now the song "I've Got No Strings" from the Disney movie *Pinocchio* is stuck in my head!)

>> **Setting the timer:** Wait — there's more, my real-life reader (another cheesy *Pinocchio* reference). You can start a recording without touching the record button! Tap the Timer icon, on the right side of the recording screen (refer to Figure 3-2). Next, tap 3s (3 seconds) or 10s (10 seconds), and then tap Start Countdown (iPhone), as shown in Figure 3-6, or Start Shooting (Android). You hear a count-down and the video starts at 0 seconds.

Using a timer is a great way to position your device in the location you want and then move to a location elsewhere in the recording screen, where viewers don't have to see you tap record during your video. You can also adjust when the recording automatically stops by sliding the vertical red bar. For example, if you want the recording to stop at 5 seconds, slide the red bar to 5 seconds. Your video now starts and stops automatically.

FIGURE 3-6:
Configuring
when to
start the
recording.

Drag to set recording limit   3s   10s

Start countdown

One of the first videos I created on this book's TikTok page (https://tiktok.com/@tiktokfordummiesbook) is a demo showing you how to quick-tap, tap-and-hold, zoom (in both methods), and use the Timer icon.

So far, I've covered three of the five icons that appear in the upper right of the recording screen: Flip, Speed, and Timer. I cover the Filters icon in its own section later in the chapter. That leaves only the Beauty icon. The Beauty effect makes your face look, well, more beautiful — if that's even possible with a beautiful face like yours! This effect can be used on top of all other effects. It smooths your skin, enhances your eyes, and does its best to make people like me look prettier during videos. Be careful, though, because some folks think it results in an unnatural look.

Picking Sounds for Your Video

TikTok is what I call a "movie studio in your pocket" (is that stuck in your head yet?) — and what professional movie production could happen without a soundtrack? Fortunately, adding a soundtrack is easy. And because TikTok's parent company, Byte-Dance, purchased the Musical.ly app in 2017, TikTok users can legally use millions of soundbites and songs! You can also use original audio for your video content, and other users can include those original sounds in their videos as well.

In the last few years, many unknown artists have posted original songs on TikTok that thousands, or even millions, of others then used in the background of their video content. These artists have gone on to produce number-one hits on radio, TV, and music apps such as Spotify and iTunes. TikTok is quickly killing the YouTube star, in the same way that MTV-style video killed the radio star — by empowering previously unknown artists to go viral! (And for those in the MTV generation that got the "Video Killed the Radio Star" reference, you now have another song by the Buggles stuck in your head — you're welcome!)

Here's how you tap into the millions of songs and soundbites available on TikTok, and use them in your own video:

1. **Before tapping record for the first time, at the top of the recording screen, tap the Sounds icon.**

    The sounds screen appears, displaying the Discover tab, as shown in Figure 3-7.

2. **To find a song or a sound-bite, type keywords in the Search field at the top or scroll through options on the Discover tab.**

The Discover tab shows you some of the top trending songs currently used in other TikTok videos:

- *Recommended (iOS) or For You (Android):* See the sounds and songs trending on TikTok that you might be interested in. Swipe left to see more recommended options.

- *Playlist:* View different categories of sounds and music you can use (which may be customized for each user), including New Releases and TikTok Viral. Tap All (iOS) or See All (Android) to scroll through a longer list.

FIGURE 3-7:
Start your song quest here.

- *Featured and beyond:* Swipe left and right to see more of what's in Featured or tap All to scroll through a list. Scroll below Featured to see more songs and sounds organized into categories such as Latin, 90s Hits, and Funky. In each category, you can swipe left to see more options or tap All or See All to scroll through a list.

3. **Tap a sound to play it.**

A red check mark appears to the right of the sound, as shown in Figure 3-8. To pause the sound, simply tap the sound again.

TIP

If you want more TikTok users to see your video, select a sound in the Recommended or Viral category.

4. **Tap the favorite icon to the right of any sound you find interesting.**

   This icon looks like a little ribbon. Any song you select appears in the Favorites tab.

5. **To use the sound in your recording, tap its red check mark.**

   You're redirected to the recording screen. When you record your video, the sound automatically plays as you record.

You can select only one sound per video. That sound will play continuously across every segment of video you record.

FIGURE 3-8:
The red check mark appears when the sound is playing.

WARNING

If you choose a sound that is shorter than your combined video length, the sound will end before the video finishes. Try to choose sounds that are at least as long as your combined video.

TIP

To add sound to, or replace sound on, an already recorded video (or one you've uploaded), go to the editing screen and tap Sounds in the lower-left corner. The added sound screen appears with two tabs (Recommended, the default, and Favorites) and a list of songs.

Tap a sound to choose it and tap Volume to adjust how loud or soft it plays, if necessary. On the Volume tab, you can also adjust your original sound as it is now mixed with the new chosen sound. If you need to trim the sound clip to match the content of your video, tap the trim icon (scissors in Android and a music note with scissors in iOS). Tap anywhere in your video above the sound choices, and then tap Next. The sound is added to the video and is ready to be posted (or saved as a draft). For details on posting, see Chapter 4.

Choosing Effects for Your Video

TikTok wouldn't be a "movie studio in your pocket" if you couldn't put on digital makeup, make your face morph into a unicorn, or turn the background into the digital fantasy world of your dreams. You can create this magical world of unicorns through the effects menu.

The effects menu enables you, the producer of your TikTok movie, to add all the smoke and mirrors you need to make your recording interesting and fun. You add these special effects through animations that recognize your face and transform you and your environment. (TikTok effects are similar to Snapchat filters.)

Here's how to explore effects and add them to your recording:

1. **Tap the + icon and then tap the Effects icon, as shown in Figure 3-9, left.**

   The effects menu appears, displaying the default Trending options, as shown in Figure 3-9, right.

   Note: You can add some but not all effects to a video you've already recorded.

FIGURE 3-9: Click the Effects icon (left) to display the effects menu (right).

2. **Check out the variety of effects:**

   - *To see all Trending effects, swipe up.*

   - *To see other effects categories, swipe left through the category names at the top. Tap a category name to see its effects. Or swipe left anywhere on the effect icons below to switch from category to category.*

   - *Tap the ribbon icon to the left of Trending to see your favorites.*

Each effect icon represents an effect. A down arrow on the icon means you haven't used it before (the arrow disappears after you tap the effect). AR in the lower left is an augmented reality effect that usually shows an animation that interacts in 3D with your environment, using special technology inside your phone. TikTok changes effects regularly, so different effects may appear on your screen than the ones shown in this section.

3. **Tap an effect to preview it.**

   Some effects include instructions, prompting you to perform actions and showing you how to use the effect. Actions for effects include gestures, such as pointing your finger at the screen to make a drum set appear and play the "Ba dum tss!" sound (see Figure 3-10, left).

   One of my favorite effects is to upload a virtual green screen, replacing everything stationary behind me in the video. For example, in Figure 3-10, right, I look like I'm walking down a street in Europe when I'm actually in my messy office.

FIGURE 3-10:
The "Ba dum tss!" effect (left) and a virtual green screen behind me (right).

4. **To save an effect for later use, make sure it's selected and then tap the favorite icon.**

   Make sure you tap the favorite icon in the lower left of the recording screen, not the favorite icon to the left of Trending (refer to Figure 3-10, left).

5. **Do one of the following:**

   - *To add your effect:* Tap outside the effects menu and then tap the Record button to start recording the next video segment with the chosen effect. If the effect requires you to use your hands or feet, make sure they're free while recording. You may need a tripod or something to prop up your device.

     - *To leave the effects menu without adding the effect to your recording:* Tap the effect a second time or tap the circle with a diagonal line (to the left of the favorite icon).

Take your time exploring the different categories of effects and learning how to use them:

>> **Trending and New:** The first category shows you what's popular, and the second shows you what's, well, new.

>> **Green Screen:** The effects here enable you to upload an image or a video to alter your surroundings in different ways. In this way, you can get creative and showcase an image or a video in your video.

>> **Interactive:** Effects here might have text (which you can customize) bubbling up on the screen or an intergalactic heart floating in the palm of your hand.

>> **Editing:** Split your screen into a grid, add staticky lines or pulsating colors to the screen, add a rainbow aura around yourself, and more.

>> **Beauty:** Virtually adding makeup to your face or changing your hair color are just two ways to enhance your look with the Beauty effects.

>> **Funny:** Turn yourself into a cartoon unicorn, hockey player, and more with the Funny effects.

>> **World:** These effects use your device to detect your surroundings so you can virtually augment the world

around you with things like cartoon objects, animals, and emojis dancing across your desk or swimming along the floor. Your device must support augmented reality for this category to appear.

>> **Animal:** Give yourself animal eyes and ears or point your camera at a cherished pet.

The more effects that you become familiar with, the more creative and unique your videos will be.

TIP

You can load multiple effects to a single video, as long as you add only one effect per clip. To load a new effect, tap the stop button to pause the recording where you want to load a new effect. Then repeat the preceding steps to choose a new effect, and tap record again to start a new clip in your recording with the new effect loaded.

Selecting a Filter for Your Video

In addition to effects to make your videos more interesting, fun, and interactive, TikTok has given your "movie studio in your pocket" multiple filters to adjust the color and lighting of your videos.

You can apply filters on top of an effect. To select a filter, follow these steps:

1. **Tap the Filters icon, on the right side of the recording screen.**

   The filters menu slides up from the bottom, as shown in Figure 3-11.

FIGURE 3-11: The filters menu shows different color filters for your video.

2. **Swipe left through the filters to explore how you can enhance your recording:**

- *Portrait:* These options work best for people.

- *Landscape:* These options are fine-tuned for videos of buildings and other structures.

- *Food:* Play with the filters here to see which one makes your freshly baked scones looked most delicious.

- *Vibe:* These filters can change the mood of your videos. Change the video to black and white, for example, to give it a noir feel, or change it to look like it was shot in the 1960s or 1970s.

- *Management:* This tool allows you to customize which filters appear when you record future videos. Use this option if you want to choose from a subset of filters instead of surfing through the entire list.

3. **Tap a filter that looks interesting.**

The filter loads in the recording screen above the filters menu, and you can see what your video looks like with the filter.

TIP

If you want to adjust the intensity of the chosen filter, move the red slider bar right or left. The slider bar appears above the filters menu when you select a filter (refer to Figure 3-11).

4. **Do one of the following:**

- *To use a filter in your recording:* Make sure the filter is selected, and tap on the recording screen to exit the filters menu. The big red record button appears again at the bottom of the recording screen, with the filter applied. In Figure 3-12, I selected the Fade filter.

FIGURE 3-12:
The recording screen, with my selected filter applied.

- *To exit the screen without using the filter:* Tap the circle with a line through it in the upper-right corner of the filters screen.

5. **When you're ready to record, tap the record button.**

   Your device starts recording with the chosen filter applied.

Recording in TikTok versus Uploading

Thus far in this chapter I've discussed recording inside the TikTok app. Guess what? (My kids and TikTok audience can hear me answering in Dad-joke fashion, "Chicken butt?") You can also upload videos and images straight from your mobile device instead of recording on-the-fly inside the app. In your device's settings, you'll have to give TikTok permission to access your videos and images.

When uploading videos versus recording in the app, you can do the following:

>> **Create videos in other apps.** By using third-party apps, you can improve the production quality of your videos.

>> **Record with professional equipment.** Take advantage of better quality cameras, microphones, and other equipment. Rather than using your phone's camera and micro-phone, you might want to use, say, a Canon or Nikon camera and a Shure SM7B microphone.

TIP

You can't attach a professional camera to your mobile device while recording, but you can attach a professional microphone to most mobile devices. The easiest method is to take the cheap wired earbuds that came with your mobile phone, attach them to the device, and use the microphone on the earbuds. Believe it or not, the result can rival professional-quality sound from much more expensive audio gear!

>> **Edit with a professional editing app.** Edit the videos you create outside TikTok on the default Photos or Videos app or any other video-editing app on your phone. You can even edit your creations on a desktop computer, using apps such as iMovie (Mac and iOS) or Adobe Premiere (most desktop operating systems).

After you've edited the video the way you like, transfer it to your mobile device. (I assume you know how to transfer videos to your device.) Then upload it to TikTok as follows:

1. **On the recording screen, tap the Upload icon, which is to the right of the record button.**

   The video selection screen appears, displaying thumbnails of all videos and images stored on your mobile device.

2. **Tap the down arrow next to All Photos at the top, and then tap the Videos tab, if necessary, to browse through your videos.**

   To browse through your photos, you'd tap the Image tab.

3. **To preview a video, tap the thumbnail — do not tap the circle in the thumbnail's upper-right corner.**

4. **To select a video on the preview screen, tap the circle to the right of Select. On the video selection screen, tap the circle in the upper-right corner of the thumbnail.**

   You can select multiple videos (and photos) to upload to become one TikTok video.

   The circle turns red (or white) and sports a number, and the selected video appears in a list of videos at the bottom of the screen, as shown in Figure 3-13.

5. **To add an image, tap the Image tab and browse your photos. Select an image by tapping the upper-right circle in the image's thumbnail.**

   Just like the video thumbnails, the image is added to the list of thumbnails at the bottom.

6. **To change the order of a photo or video in the list, drag it to a new location.**

   You can change the order also on the editing screen.

7. **To delete a thumbnail in the list, tap the X icon in the thumbnail's upper right.**

   In Chapter 4, I show you how to edit the duration of any thumbnail selected here. You can also add sound effects, text, and icons after you upload.

8. **After your selected videos and photos are in the correct order, tap the Next button in the lower right (refer to Figure 3-13).**

   You're taken to the editing screen, where you can do post editing.

In Chapter 4, I show you what you can do with videos and images recorded inside the TikTok app before you finally publish to your audience.

FIGURE 3-13:
Selected videos appear at the bottom.

Using Templates to Show Off Your Photos

In the preceding section, you added photos to your video by tapping the Upload icon on the recording screen. If you want, you can use these photos to create a slideshow instead. TikTok makes the process easy by providing a series of templates.

To create a photo slideshow template:

1. **On the recording screen, tap Templates at the bottom of the screen.**

   The templates screen appears, showcasing a sample template using TikTok's stock photography and music, as shown in

Figure 3-14. At the top is the template's title (Film in this example) and the maximum number of photos you can use in the template.

2. **To browse the templates, swipe left.**

   As you swipe, each template automatically loads a preview with stock pictures and music.

3. **When you find a template you like, tap the Select Photos button below the preview.**

   The select photos screen appears, as shown in Figure 3-15, so you can select the photos to add to your template straight from your device's storage.

FIGURE 3-14:
The templates screen.

FIGURE 3-15:
The select photos screen.

4. **Tap the upper-right circle of each photo you want to include, up to the maximum number of photos allowed for your chosen template.**

The circle turns red or white with a number, and the photo thumbnail appears in a list at the bottom of the screen, just like in the video selection screen described in the preceding section.

5. **To preview a photo in the list, tap the thumbnail.**

Do not tap the X in the corner of the thumbnail, because doing so will remove the photo from the list.

6. **To reorder a thumbnail in the list, drag it to the desired order and then tap OK.**

The photo slideshow appears in the editing screen, as shown in Figure 3-16. Congrats — you just turned a list of still photos into an interesting and pretty video with music of your favorite photos and images!

FIGURE 3-16:
The editing screen with your loaded template.

On the editing screen, you can change the sounds and effects, add text and stickers, and more. You can also save your video as a draft, to be edited and posted later. I show you how to do this and more in Chapter 4.

IN THIS CHAPTER

» **Editing recorded clips**

» **Adding pizzaz with filters, effects, text, and stickers**

» **Including sound post recording**

» **Adding a description and hashtags and adjusting privacy settings**

» **Taking your video live**

Chapter **4**

Publishing Your TikTok Video

I f you've just finished recording on the recording screen, you're probably eager to get the video to a wider audience. However, before I take you there, you might enjoy knowing that you can do more with that video. In this chapter, I show you the many ways you can edit a video after recording. Then you see how to publish your video.

REMEMBER

You can edit videos you've saved to your Drafts folder: From your profile page, tap Drafts, and then tap the video you want to edit. On the post screen that appears, tap the back arrow in the upper-left corner to go to the editing screen.

Adjusting Clip Size after Recording

After you finish recording a video inside the TikTok app, the editing screen appears, as shown in Figure 4-1, so you can edit the video before publishing it. For example, you can adjust the size of each individual clip, reshoot clips, and even rearrange them.

What individual clips, you ask? TikTok enables you to pause and restart video recording (see Chapter 3) to add various effects and filters or to just, say, go into another room. As you do so, those clips are saved as discrete pieces of the video that you can edit individually.

REMEMBER

The option to adjust clips is available only for videos recorded inside the TikTok app — not those recorded elsewhere and uploaded to TikTok. If you recorded the video natively in the TikTok app, you can use the adjust clips feature shown in the following steps.

FIGURE 4-1:
The editing screen.

To adjust the clips you just recorded:

1. **Tap the Adjust Clips icon in the upper-right of the editing screen, under the Filters icon (refer to Figure 4-1).**

   The full-sized video appears, playing automatically, as shown in Figure 4-2. Tap the video to pause it, and then tap it again to resume. At the bottom of the screen is the adjust clips menu. A red box displays your entire recorded video, and below that are your previously recorded individual clips.

A clip is an individual segment of your entire recorded video. To record a clip, go to the recording screen and either tap and hold while recording, or tap to record and then tap to stop. The video is added as a clip to your full recording. Repeat this as often as time allows to add more clips to your full video.

2. **To rerecord a clip:**

   a. *Tap the individual clip you'd like to edit.* The edit clip menu appears, as shown in Figure 4-3.

   b. *Tap Start Over (iOS) or the camera icon with the arrow (Android).* A new recording screen appears. Chapter 3 covers recording videos using this screen in detail.

FIGURE 4-2:
The adjust clips menu.

   c. *Record as many new clips as you want within the time frame of the individual clip you're editing.* The clips will be added to the full video. The replacement clips must use up the same total amount of time as the clips they are replacing. You'll know this is the case when the check mark next to the record button turns red.

   d. *Tap the red check mark.* If you recorded multiple clips to replace the original clip, the adjust clips menu reappears, with your newly recorded clips in order. If you recorded one continuous clip to replace the original clip, an adjustment menu for that clip appears.

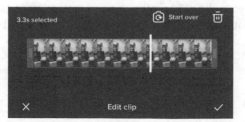

FIGURE 4-3:
The edit clip menu.

3. **To delete a clip:**

   a. *Tap the clip you want to delete.*

   b. *Tap the trash can icon next to the Start Over icon.*

   c. *When prompted, tap Delete.* The adjust clips menu reappears.

4. **To trim the length of a clip:**

   a. *Select the clip and move the red box surrounding the bar at the bottom.* On the left and right side of the red box are three small, white vertical lines (refer to Figure 4-3). When you drag these, your clip is shortened from the beginning (drag left) or the end (drag right). You can shorten a clip to a minimum of .5 second. The length of your clip appears on the left above the red slider box.

   b. *After you have selected your desired clip length, tap the check mark icon in the lower right to save your clip.* The adjust clips menu appears, showing all your clips together as one video.

   To undo all your changes to the clip, tap the X icon in the lower left.

5. **To trim the length of the entire video, drag the three vertical lines on the left and right of the red box at the bottom, just as you did for an individual clip in Step 4.**

6. **To save your changes, tap Save.**

   You return to the editing screen.

You've now created perfectly timed clips to compile a nice, smooth video!

TIP

Sometimes it's fun to combine the adjust clips feature in this chapter with the timer feature on the recording screen in Chapter 3. Tap the Timer icon on the recording screen, and drag the red vertical bar on the screen that appears to the intended length of your clip. When your clip automatically starts, it records only to that intended length, saving the need to adjust clips later!

Adding Filters and Effects to Recorded Videos

You've cropped, adjusted, and edited all the clips you want to with the adjust clips feature (see the preceding section). However, the editing screen allows you to make a few more minor visual adjustments to your fully recorded video by using filters and effects.

TIP

The filters and effects that you can add after recording inside the TikTok app (or uploading from elsewhere) are different before recording than after recording. I recommend adding as many visual effects and filters as possible when you're recording (or through your own video editing software if you're uploading a recording to TikTok), because many of those are not available on the editing screen.

Adding filters after recording

As mentioned, TikTok enables you to add filters to your videos after recording. On the editing screen, tap the Filters icon. The filters are the same as the ones on the recording screen, which I describe in Chapter 3. Refer to that chapter as needed to learn how to use filters with your videos here.

Adding effects after recording

As mentioned, the same filters are available whether you're recording or have finished recording. However, you have a few different options when adding effects after recording than while recording. To access these additional effects:

1. **At the bottom of the editing screen, tap the Effects icon.**

   Your recorded video appears at the top, as shown in Figure 4-4. Below that is the new effects menu, which contains a slider bar indicating what part of the video is currently playing. At the bottom are different categories, with the Visual category selected by default. Above the categories are the visual effects in that category.

2. **Explore the new effects menu to get an idea of what you can do here.**

Tap the play icon (triangle) to play your recorded video. Then drag the vertical white line in the slider bar to move within the video. Drag across the circles below that to explore the effects available in the selected category.

3. **On the slider bar below the main video, drag the white vertical line to the spot where you want to add an effect.**

The main video fast-forwards or reverses to the location you choose.

TIP

You can instead play the video until it gets to the desired location in your video, at which point you tap the video again to pause it.

FIGURE 4-4: The new effects menu on the editing screen, with the Transition category selected.

4. **Tap the category and then do the following:**

- *Visual:* This effect is loaded by default when you open the new effects menu. Press one of the circles at the bottom (such as Smog, Flower, or Gold Powder) to start the effect, and release when you want the effect to stop. The effect appears over your video as it plays, so you can see what the effect looks like (see Figure 4-5). To delete the effect, tap the curved undo icon.

- *Effects:* This category provides a limited number of effects, compared to what's available while recording. Tap an effect to see what it looks like in your video. The effects in this category are applied to the entire video. To delete the effect, tap it a second time to remove it.

REMEMBER

You can choose only one effect from the Effects category to apply to your video, but it can appear on top of effects from other categories.

- *Transition:* You use transition effects to add transitions (such as a slide, fade out, or fade in) from frame to frame at different parts of your video. Press one of the circles to add a transition effect at the location you chose in Step 3. To delete the effect, tap the curved undo icon.

- *Split:* Press one of the circles to apply the effect at the selected location. The effect carves your screen into multiple parts, adding a fun split-screen effect. To delete the effect, tap the curved undo icon.

FIGURE 4-5:
Applying an effect to your recorded video.

- *Time:* You can display special time warp options that apply reversal, repetition, and even slow-motion effects to your video. Choose a location and then press the circle to apply the effect. To remove the effect, tap the not symbol to the left of the options.

5. **Tap the Save button in the upper right to save your effects.**

   If you don't want to save your effects, tap Cancel in the upper left. You return to the editing screen, with the new effects applied (or not) to the recorded video.

Adding Sound to Recorded Videos

For the most professional videos, adding the appropriate sounds and music as background and foreground is important! As you learn in Chapter 2, you can search by specific sounds in the videos of other users, so the sounds and music you choose can also help people discover your videos more easily.

Using sounds from TikTok

If you didn't already choose music for your video while you were recording in the TikTok app, you can still add sound and music to the background of your video, straight from TikTok. And if you already chose music for your video, you can also still edit and replace the sounds and music right on the editing screen.

To add or edit music and sounds, follow these steps:

1. **In the lower left of the editing screen, tap Sounds.**

   The sounds menu slides up, displaying recommended sounds (in squares), as shown in Figure 4-6. (The Recommended tab is selected by default.) If you chose a sound as you were recording in TikTok, that sound would be selected and would repeat over and over.

FIGURE 4-6: The sounds menu.

2. **Preview some sounds:**

   a. *Drag your finger along the list to see all suggested songs.*

   b. *Tap a sound to select it and hear it on repeat. Tap again to stop the song.*

   c. *Tap the Favorites tab to see sounds or songs you've bookmarked.*

3. **Tap the Recommended tab, if necessary, and then tap More to explore more sounds.**

   The sounds screen appears. Refer to Chapter 3 to learn how to find, select, and mark as favorites additional sounds to use in your video. If you select a sound on this screen, you return to the previous screen with the selected sound loaded on repeat.

4. **Adjust the volume as follows:**

   a. *Tap Volume.* The volume menu appears (see Figure 4-7), where you can adjust the volume of the original sound of your recorded video and the sound you selected.

   b. *Drag the sliders to turn the volume up or down.* The new volume is applied to the video, which plays on repeat.

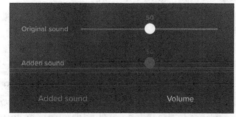

FIGURE 4-7:
The volume menu.

5. **Adjust which part of the sound plays:**

   a. *Tap Added Sound and then tap the crop icon (musical note and scissors or just scissors) in the upper right.* The crop menu appears, displaying white vertical lines that change to blue lines as the video plays. See Figure 4-8.

   b. *To select the part of the audio that you want to play in your video, drag the vertical lines left or right.*

6. **To save your changes, tap the red check mark in the lower right.**

That's it — your sound should be playing in the desired location in your video. To get back to the editing screen, tap anywhere on the main video, outside the sounds menu.

Adding voiceover and narration

For some video styles, you may want to record the visual parts of the video first and add sound later. This option works great when you want to add narration on top of the video, for instance. You can do this after you record in TikTok or upload your initial video.

To add a voiceover or narration to your recorded video, go to the editing screen for that video and follow these steps:

Courtesy of Katelyn Handy (@katelyn_handy)

FIGURE 4-8:
The crop menu.

1. **Tap the Voiceover icon (microphone).**

   Your recorded video appears, as shown in Figure 4-9. The voiceover menu is at the bottom, with a slider box for choosing where in the video you'll add voiceover sounds or narration as well as a record button (white circle with a red dot).

2. **Drag the white vertical line in the slider box to the location where you want to add a voiceover.**

   The video at the top fast-forwards or reverses to that location.

3. **To begin your voiceover, tap the record button and begin speaking into your mobile device. Tap again to stop the recording.**

   You can also long-press the button to record (and release the button to stop). As you record, the vertical white line slides to the right. When you finish recording, the area you recorded over is marked in red in the slider box.

4. **To review what you just recorded, drag the vertical white line to the area you just recorded, and tap the play icon.**

   To discard the audio you just recorded, tap the undo icon (curved arrow).

5. **Repeat Steps 3 and 4 until you're satisfied with your voiceover.**

6. **Tap Save in the upper right.**

   The editing screen appears with your new voiceover applied.

FIGURE 4-9: The voiceover menu.

TIP

If you want only your voiceover, without the original sound that was recorded with the video, tap to deselect Keep Original Sound.

At this point, your video is repeating on the editing screen, with your new voiceover playing on top. To adjust the volume of your voiceover, see the steps in the preceding section, "Using sounds from TikTok."

Adding voice effects

In videos where you or others are talking — including voiceovers — you can alter the voice of the main person speaking. Use this feature to create fun effects, such as making the speaker sound like a chipmunk or a robot.

To add voice effects to your video, follow these steps from the editing screen:

1. **Tap the voice effects icon in the upper right.**

   The voice effects menu appears, as shown in Figure 4-10.

FIGURE 4-10:
The voice
effects
menu.

2. **Swipe left and right in the list of voice effects at the bottom.**

3. **Tap the desired voice effect.**

   The primary voice in the video changes to the selected voice effect, and the video repeats continuously using that effect. You can choose only one effect to use in the entire video.

4. **Repeat Steps 2 and 3 to experiment with other voice effects.**

   Tap None at the far left to choose no voice effects.

5. **When you're happy with your chosen voice effect, tap outside the voice effects menu to return to the editing screen.**

TIP

Refer to the voice effects menu often to see if new effects have been added. Being one of the first to use a new feature on TikTok can bring more attention to your video!

Adding Text and Stickers to Recorded Videos

Your video is looking and sounding fine, and you could publish it the way it is. But if you think it needs a little something extra, TikTok's text and stickers features might come in handy. You can add text, stickers, and animated graphics to any part of your video, adding a pop of personality and spunk to make the video more appealing.

Adding text

Adding text is easy, and there's a lot you can do with it. Text makes your videos more accessible to those who are hard of hearing and gives TikTok data it can use to tell those who are sight impaired what is happening in your videos (if they have special settings enabled on their device). Text also makes things stand out, giving you another way to convey your video's message.

To add and edit text throughout your video:

1. **Tap the Text icon at the bottom of the editing screen.**

   Your recorded video continues to repeat while a blinking red cursor and keyboard appear, along with a series of font, alignment, color, and background options, as shown in Figure 4-11.

   FIGURE 4-11:
   The edit text menu.

2. **Type text using the keyboard.**

   Your text, in the default Classic font, appears in white over the playing video.

3. **Select the font to use for the text you typed in Step 2.**

   Slide Classic to see other options, including Typewriter, Handwriting, and Serif. Your text changes to the chosen font.

4. **Tap the alignment icon (horizontal white lines) until your text is aligned the way you want.**

   Text defaults to centered, but you can set it to left align or right align.

5. **Tap a colored circle to choose that color for your text.**

   Your text changes to the selected color. To see more color options, slide the colored circles left or right.

6. **Tap A (the leftmost icon) to choose a background for your text.**

   Your choices are no background (the default,) a solid outline around letters, a solid-colored rectangular background, and a translucent rectangular background. Background styles and availability vary depending on the font and color you choose.

7. **When your text looks how you want, tap Done in the upper right of the screen.**

   You return to the editing screen.

Your text appears in the center of your video throughout the entire length of the video. What if you want to move the text, edit it, or change when it appears? It's simple.

FIGURE 4-12:
These options appear next to text you want to change.

First tap the text you want to change. A new set of options appears, as shown in Figure 4-12.

TIP

To delete the text instead of changing it, drag the text upwards and into the trash can that appears. The text is gone forever.

To enable a computer-generated voice, tap Text-to-Speech. A robotic-sounding voice will read the selected text when it appears. Use this feature to describe the video for viewers with vision difficulties.

To change how long the text appears onscreen, do the following:

1. **Tap Set Duration.**

   The screen shown in Figure 4-13 appears, with your video at the top and the duration menu with the familiar slider box at the bottom.

2. **To change when the text first appears, drag the left side of the red box (the three small white vertical lines) to the right.**

   The video fast-forwards and rewinds as you slide the box, with your text appearing at the leftmost part of the red box. To play the video from the current location, tap the white play triangle below the main video. To pause the video, tap the white triangle again.

FIGURE 4-13:
The duration menu.

3. **To change when the text disappears, slide the right side of the red slider box.**

   The video fast-forwards and rewinds as before, showing the spot where the text ends.

4. **To see where the text appears and disappears, slide the large white vertical location marker on the slider box backwards and forwards.**

   As you slide the white location marker left and right, the video fast-forwards and rewinds. When it passes the left side of the red box, the text appears, and when it passes the right side of the red box, the text disappears. Be sure to adjust the red box if your text is appearing and disappearing in the wrong place.

5. **Tap the play icon (white triangle) to play and pause the video.**

   Ensure that the text appears and disappears in the correct location.

6. **To save your changes, tap the check mark in the lower right.**

   Or tap the X in the lower left to cancel your changes. The editing screen appears with your changes implemented (or not).

You can add as many pieces of text as you want to your video at this point. Repeat the preceding steps for each piece of text.

You can edit your text at any time by simply tapping the text and then tapping Edit in the menu that appears (refer to Figure 4-12).

TIP

As mentioned, you can add text describing what is happening or being said in your video (called closed captioning). Want automatic closed captioning? Check out the third-party app called Captions for TikTok, available in your device's app store. You can upload any video to the Captions for TikTok app and automatically use speech recognition to add closed captioning to your TikTok videos.

Adding stickers and emojis

You can also add stickers and emojis that appear and disappear in your video. After you select a sticker or emoji, you edit it and set its duration in the same way you do with text. In the following steps, I show you how to find a sticker and place it in your video. The steps for using an emoji are similar:

1. **At the bottom of the editing screen, tap the Stickers icon.**

   The screen shown in Figure 4-14, left, appears, displaying the Stickers tab. Tap the other tab, Emojis, if you want to add an emoji to a video.

2. **To search for a sticker, scroll up and down through the recommended options or type a keyword in the Search box.**

   Stickers related to your keyword appear. I typed **Follow** in Figure 4-14, right.

FIGURE 4-14:
Scroll
through the
stickers
(left) or
type a
keyword to
search
(right).

3. **Tap a sticker to add it to your video.**

   The sticker appears In the center of your video, and the stickers screen disappears.

4. **To adjust the location of your sticker, long-press it and move it.**

5. **Adjust the size and orientation of the sticker, if desired.**

   Press down on the sticker with two fingers. Then pinch your fingers to shrink the sticker, spread them to enlarge the sticker, or twist them right or left to rotate the sticker.

To delete the sticker, drag the sticker to the trash can.

Pinning stickers, emojis, and text

You can also set, or *pin,* a sticker, emoji, or text to an object or a person so that it follows that object or person around the screen. To pin a sticker, follow these steps:

1. **Tap the sticker once.**

2. **In the screen that appears, tap Pin.**

   The pin screen appears, as shown in Figure 4-15.

   Note: Instead of tapping Pin after tapping the sticker, tap Set Duration to set when and how long the sticker appears in your video, the same way you did for text earlier in the chapter. Refer to the steps for setting text duration in the "Adding text" section.

3. **Drag the white slider at the bottom of the screen to the point in the video where you want to pin the sticker.**

4. **Adjust the size and rotation of the sticker, if desired.**

   Refer to the steps in the preceding section for details.

5. **Tap Pin at the bottom.**

   The editing screen appears with your video playing and the sticker following your chosen object (or person).

FIGURE 4-15:
The pin screen.

Publishing Your Video

When you've finished editing, it's time for the final steps in publishing your video to an audience! You can set your audience, add a description, and adjust other settings for your recording on the post screen, shown in Figure 4-16. To get there, tap the Next button in the lower right of the editing screen.

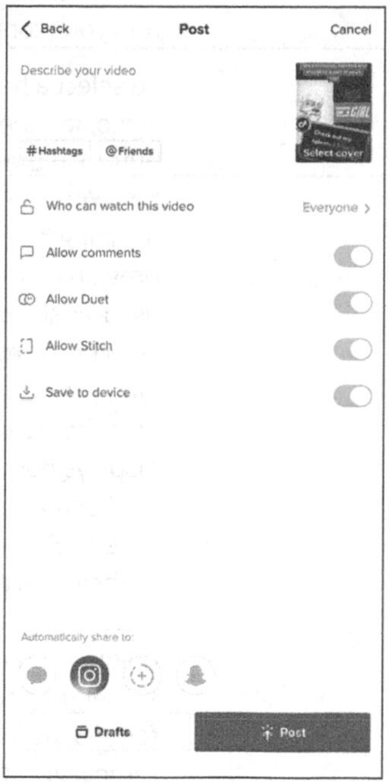

REMEMBER

You don't have to post a video right after recording and editing it. Instead, you can save it to Drafts by tapping the Drafts button to the left of the Post button. To access videos in Drafts, go to your profile page and tap Drafts. Want to edit a video before posting? Tap the video, and you're taken to the post screen; tap Back in the upper left, and you're on the editing screen. To delete a video in the Drafts folder, swipe left on the video and tap Delete.

FIGURE 4-16: The post screen.

Creating a description and tagging

To ensure that your content gets discovered, liked, and shared, type a relevant, short description for your video in the Describe Your Video section at the top of the post screen. Following are suggestions for writing a description that's easy for others to discover:

>> **Be brief.** Descriptions can be no longer than 150 characters. Your description should be a quick summary to further get your audience interacting, commenting, and engaging with your video. TikTok users have short attention spans, so short is good!

>> **Use at least one hashtag.** Hashtags tell TikTok which audiences to show your videos to. In addition, as I describe in Chapter 2, hashtags can be a great way to help users find your content in searches and popular memes.

To select a hashtag for your video, tap the #Hashtags button in the Description box. You see a list of trending hashtags and previous hashtags you've used, as shown in Figure 4-17. Select one from the list, or type your own, starting with the # symbol. TikTok displays how many views the hashtag is getting by others who have added it to their descriptions. If you added an effect or another unique element, TikTok sometimes adds a hashtag for you, which you can remove if you want.

FIGURE 4-17:
A list of hashtags appears.

Many users add the hashtag #FYP (For You Page) because they think it will make their video more likely to appear on the For You page of other users. My research shows that this doesn't affect your videos one way or another, so save the precious character count and leave it out!

>> **Tag friends and influencers.** To tag people in your description, tap the @Friends button in the Description box or type the @ symbol, followed by the username of each account you want to tag. When you publish the video, those people will get a notification that they were tagged, giving them a reason to comment, like, share, or even follow your account.

Tagging too many people in a description or tagging one person too often is considered spammy and bad etiquette. It's also a good way to get your account blocked by the person or ignored by those you're tagging. See Chapter 5 for more on TikTok etiquette.

To get a list of hashtags that will work best for your video, use an app such as my personal favorite, Hashtag Expert, available in all the app stores. This app lists suggested hashtags that it detects are performing well on TikTok, based on keywords you enter in the app. I copy my favorites and paste them in my description before I publish my videos.

Editing the cover image

After you have a unique description optimized for maximum visibility, you should edit the cover animation or image that appears when people view your profile page. This image appears also if people share your video as a link on other platforms on the Internet. To edit your cover image:

1. **In the video thumbnail in the upper right of the post screen, tap Select Cover.**

   The top animated image in your cover image appears, as shown in Figure 4-18, left. Next is the cover image menu, with a slider box so you can scroll through videos to get to the right spot quickly. Below the slider box is a list of text art styles you can add to the cover image.

   The Select Cover text is really small, and it's easy to tap the wrong part of the thumbnail. If you tap the top part of the cover image, you'll see a preview screen instead of the screen in Figure 4-18, left. Tap the preview screen to go back to the post screen.

2. **Drag the slider box until you find the frame that you want as your thumbnail image.**

   The main cover image at the top moves forward and backward as you drag. After you release your finger, the main image remains animated, repeating a two- or three-frame clip from that spot.

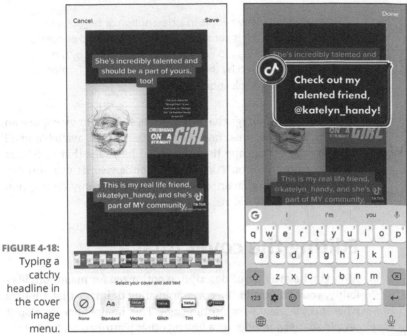

FIGURE 4-18:
Typing a catchy headline in the cover image menu.

3. **Type your text:**

   a. *Swipe left on the text art styles at the bottom and then tap the one you like.* After you select a style, it overlays the main image at the top, with a cursor prompting you to add text.

   b. *Type a headline in the box that appears (see Figure 4-18, right).* Type something catchy — remember, the text will appear on your profile, and you want your profile visitors to know why they should watch this video!

   c. *Tap Done in the upper right.*

4. **Adjust the size and orientation of the text, if necessary.**

   To do so, long-press the text with two fingers. Then spread your fingers to expand the text, pinch your fingers to shrink it, or rotate and move your fingers to reposition it.

5. **To save your changes, tap Save in the upper-right corner of the screen.**

   To discard your changes, tap cancel in the upper left. Either way, the post screen appears.

SCHEDULE VIDEOS TO POST LATER

You can upload videos and then schedule them to be posted later (at least 15 minutes in the future). To access this feature, go to tiktok.com in a separate web browser, log in to your account, and tap the cloud icon in the upper-right corner. You can add a caption, choose a cover image, and decide who can view the video and what viewers can do (comment, and so on). Click the Schedule Video toggle to allow videos to be posted, and a calendar and digital clock appear. Choose a date and time (in military time) and click Schedule.

Setting privacy and sharing

After your description and cover image are set, you can tap Post and publish your video. But wait! By not looking over the privacy settings and preferences for the video, you could compromise the level of privacy you're comfortable with and not allow enough ways for others to see your video. In the following list, I note each option's default. Refer to Chapter 6 to learn how to change these defaults in your privacy settings:

>> **Who Can Watch This Video (Everyone/Followers):** This option defaults to Everyone, unless your account is set as a private account in your profile settings, in which case it defaults to Followers. Tap Everyone or Followers to choose from three choices:

- *Everyone/Followers:* Anyone on TikTok can see the video (Everyone) or only followers can see the video (Followers).

- *Friends:* Only followers you follow back can see the video.

- *Private:* Only you can see the video.

>> **Allow Comments (On):** Followers can comment on your video. See Chapter 6 for reasons why you might want to turn off this setting.

>> **Allow Duet (Off):** When this setting is turned On, people can create duets, in which they appear in a video next to yours that plays to their own audience. If you want more viewers, use the On setting. Learn more about duets in Chapter 9.

>> **Allow Stitch (Off):** When this feature is set to On, your followers can share your video to their own audiences — but only as a short blip followed by a video of their own responding to your video. The On setting drives more attention to your video. See Chapter 2 for details.

>> **Save to Device (On):** A copy of your video is automatically downloaded to your device, so you can use the video elsewhere or have a backup copy.

>> **Automatically Share to (Nothing):** Near the bottom of the post screen are icons for sharing your video via SMS (text bubble), as an Instagram post, as an Instagram story, and to Snapchat. Tap Post, and then tap an icon to open and share in the selected app. You can select only one option. These options vary based on apps that TikTok detects are installed on your phone. You may see different apps than the ones that appear in the examples.

After you've reviewed all the listed privacy and sharing options and made your selections, and you feel that your video is ready to go live, just tap the Post button in the lower right.

Congratulations! You just published your own TikTok video!

Chapter **5**

Acclimating to TikTok Etiquette and Culture

ike others in my generation — the brief generation known as xennials, for those born on the cusp between Gen X (born in the 1960s and 1970s) and the millennials (born in the 1980s or 1990s) — I've become adept at adapting to ever-changing tech cultures and jargon. After all, we invented the familiar LOLs and BRBs of AOL Instant Messenger, along with social media emojis and other forms of shortened communication styles.

Now my kids, who are in Gen Z (born in the late 1990s and early 2000s), are claiming new forms of communication, much of it gaining popularity on TikTok. TikTok culture is shaping the way we, their parents and grandparents, have to learn to communicate with them. No cap! 🚫💨 (I explain that last term, shortly.)

In this chapter, I show you the many ways TikTok is changing our culture, and how you can fit into this crazy new world I've come to love.

Becoming Familiar with TikTok Culture

TikTok has developed a different culture than other social networks you may be used to, such as Facebook or Twitter. You'll be most successful understanding this culture when you begin creating content on the platform. The key to understanding TikTok's culture is to know these principles:

>> **You're not alone!** TikTok has an estimated 1.1 billion users. (A second version of TikTok, called Douyin, is available only in China.) You'll find thriving communities in just about any genre and interest you can think of, including religion, mental health, sports, music, arts, crafts, and cooking. For example, popular TikTok user @catieosaurus uses her TikTok account to talk about ADHD, as shown in Figure 5-1. I share some of my other favorite accounts in Chapters 12 and 13.

>> **TikTok is about being yourself.** Many popular accounts convey the person's normal, everyday life. Big-name celebrities, such as Andy Grammer, use TikTok to share the behind-the-scenes of their

Courtesy of Catie O (@catieosaurus)

FIGURE 5-1: @catieosaurus highlights living with ADHD.

everyday lives. Chef Gordon Ramsey's daughter pranks her dad (he goes along with it!) for the world to see. On TikTok, everyone is human. You get to be as well.

>> **TikTok is one very large conversation.** The comment, like, duet, and stitch features get people interacting in fun and creative ways. For example, popular influencers might start a dance, or begin a conversation, or sing a song and ask their audiences to join in. (An *influencer* is a person on social media with many followers or the ability to make content go viral and even affect product purchases.) As you surf the For You page, you might discover one of their followers joining in, and get inspired to do your own creative twist for your own audience. Your audience comments and participates themselves, and the conversation continues. You can also use hashtags so that the conversation you're participating in is categorized with similar videos.

>> **TikTok is about creativity and having fun!** TikTok's mission statement is, "TikTok is the leading destination for short-form mobile video. Our mission is to inspire creativity and bring joy." As you create content on the TikTok platform, don't assume that you have to know how to dance, sing, or draw. Think about what you have to offer that is unique and creative and might spark joy in whoever watches and interacts with your content. For example, Aaron Hanania, shown in Figure 5-2, spreads positivity to his audience. Most importantly, have fun! A welcoming community is there to cheer you on.

Courtesy of Aaron Hanania (@aaronhanania)

FIGURE 5-2: @aaronhanania sparking joy in his audience.

There you go! I now dub thee, Sir or Madame (or whatever your preferred royal pronoun) reader, a part of the TikTok culture.

Speaking TikTok Jargon

Knowing a little TikTok jargon can help you sound like one of the cool kids. Trust me on this.

Here are some of the top TikTok slang words and jargon you might come across as you're using the app. Many of these are used by Gen Z, so when I'm in doubt, I just ask my kids (sheesh, I feel old):

TIP

>> *X* **TikTok:** When creators say they've stumbled upon Dog TikTok, or Cat TikTok, or TikTok For Dummies TikTok or any other number of TikToks, they're talking about a specific group or community of people with similar interests.

Usage: "Congratulations, you've stumbled upon Fruit Snack TikTok, where all your Fruit Snack cravings can come true!"

Using the *X* TikTok verbiage can be a great way to encourage your audience to join your club of followers obsessed with something as silly as fruit snacks. They might even make their own videos and duets about the exclusive club you've created.

>> **Cap (🧢) or No Cap (🚫🧢):** These were popularized by the song "No Cap" by rappers Young Thug & Future in 2017. Cap (designated by a baseball cap emoji) means lie. No Cap (designated by the prohibited emoji followed by the baseball cap) means no lie or for real. You often see the emojis used in comments if someone agrees (the no cap emoji sequence) or doesn't believe you (the cap emoji).

Usage: "No cap! TikTok For Dummies will teach anyone how to get acclimated to TikTok!" (See what I did there?)

>> **Extra:** When someone's a little *extra*, they're being overly dramatic or over-the-top.

Usage: "David seems to get into everyone's business and always wants to be the center of attention. He's so extra!"

>> **Simp:** The original Gen Z users started using TikTok to meet and date other users. They're all about flirting, and

simp is a term that means someone is doing too much for another person he or she likes.

Usage: "She's such a simp towards Allen. He doesn't even give her much, but she can't stop trying to please him!"

» **Karen:** A *Karen* is a woman who gets in everyone's business, feeling she's entitled to do so. The male equivalent is a *Chad*.

Usage: "He's such a Chad — he thinks he runs this town, reporting every violation he can find!"

» **Bet:** Short for *you bet* or *sure.* It means you acknowledge what's being said.

Usage: Person 1: "Y'all better finish reading this book soon so I can read it next!" Person 2: "Bet."

» **Thirst trap:** You'll see this term a lot on TikTok. When people create a post solely to get attention from those who might be attracted to them, it's called a *thirst trap.*

Usage: "Ha! This video is such a thirst trap. Look at all the guys simping on her!"

» **Sus:** If you're familiar with the popular computer game Among Us, you'll recognize this term, which suggests someone is suspicious. On TikTok, it's used anytime something seems suspicious.

Usage: "I don't know — this video seems a bit sus. I think that hair looks like a wig."

» **Boomer:** Originally used to define people in the baby boomer generation, *boomer* now means someone deemed too old for a younger person to grasp.

Usage (I'm quoting my kids here): "You're such a boomer, Dad. You don't even understand what sus means."

» **Yeet:** This term is used to convey excitement, approval, surprise, or just energy.

Usage: "Can't wait for my mom to get on TikTok! Yeet yeet!"

» **Clown emoji (🤡):** Appearing in comments, this term usually means something is foolish, scary, or suspicious. It's usually not a positive term.

Usage: Person 1: "I'm going to climb up this rock wall." Person 2: "🤡"

Knowing When to Like, Follow, or Share

The best way to feel part of the community is to make yourself known through liking videos that resonate with you, following users who share things you like, and showing you care about those conversations and content by sharing them with your audience in a creative way. Every time you do one of these things, it appears in the inbox notifications of the creator who made the content you're engaging with. Good listeners will recognize you as part of that community.

In this section, I show you how to use the like, follow, and share features, which I describe in more detail in Chapter 2. You might want to consider using like, follow, and share to make yourself known in the following situations:

>> **A creator says something that resonates with you:** Show the creator your appreciation by liking or commenting. You might even want to duet the video (see Figure 5-3) to add your take on the content. (For more on duets, see Chapter 9.) If you're not following the creator yet, tap Follow!

>> **Someone tags you or duets you in a video:** It's good karma and good etiquette to respond to anyone who tags you, be it in a comment or in the post of another video.

Courtesy of Marcel Roston @grayhairwhere

FIGURE 5-3: @grayhairwhere duets to respond to another influencer.

TIP

Tagging a large influencer with a lot of followers is a great way to get the person's attention. Doing so sends an extra notification to the creator, increasing the chances that he or she will see it.

>> **You find a topic that's a big part of your life:** If you see a video from someone talking about a topic you're passionate about, perhaps something you didn't realize other people felt strongly about, like that sucker! Consider leaving a comment with your experience, so the person knows he or she is not alone. And be sure to follow the person.

>> **You're trying to get on the radar of someone you find interesting or influential:** The best way to get people to show interest in you is to show genuine interest in them, with no expectation of receiving anything in return. Liking and commenting on a video or the more powerful duetting and stitching result in more people seeing that video. It's a small gesture that can make the user more popular. I discuss this approach in more detail in the next section.

>> **A video sparks an interest- ing or creative idea that would be better as a duet or stitch:** We've all watched videos where only part of the person's body is visible. Grab the opportunity to create your own version of the video by duetting. If, say, you see the person from the waist up, duet with your legs below the person's body, doing funny things as the video plays. Browse TikTok for other chances to extend someone's existing video through a duet or stitch and make it your own. You might end up producing your own viral sensation!

Courtesy of Katelyn Handy @katelyn_handy

FIGURE 5-4: @katelyn_handy duetting one of her favorite musicians.

TIP

Are you a musician? Make yourself known by finding and duetting other musicians, as shown in Figure 5-4. Many musicians have become sensations themselves because they duetted a well-known musician or influencer and that person gave them recognition for an amazing duet.

Winning Friends and Influencing People

Whenever I think about how to win friends and influence people, I think of the popular book of the same name by Dale Carnegie. In it, he teaches how to be popular by genuinely being kind and showing interest in other people, with no expectation of anything in return. When you're trying to grow an audience and influence others or get on the radar of influencers, the principals taught by Dale Carnegie still apply.

TIP

For homework, buy a copy of *How to Win Friends and Influence People* by Dale Carnegie (Pocket Books). This is a must-read for TikTokers!

Catching the attention of major influencers

Let's face it: Part of TikTok's allure is the possibility of getting lots of followers and even interacting with famous people. Although becoming popular should never be the goal for anything in life, there's value in connecting and networking with others who have an influential presence on TikTok.

The following list highlights a few reasons you might want to get on the radar of popular TikTok influencers:

>> The more they see your videos, the more likely they are to duet, stitch, or bring attention and credibility to your own videos.

>> The For You page algorithm gives your account more weight, showing it to more people, if a lot of influencers are following you and interacting with your content.

>> An influencer mentioning your TikTok account can potentially bring thousands of followers to your account.

>> When an influencer openly interacts with you, your viewers and the influencer's viewers put you on the same level as the influencer.

Helping other TikTokers

If you remember nothing else about gaining the attention of TikTok influencers, remember this: Follow the Golden Rule ("Do unto others as you would have them do unto you"). Some call this karma. Here are some ways to use this philosophy and garner the attention of influencers:

>> **Engage:** Influencers love their followers. You can't get their attention if you don't follow them first! Then like and comment their content as much as you can. Mention them in your comments for more attention. If they share their birthday anywhere (please don't stalk them), wish them a happy birthday when the day arrives.

>> **Duet and stitch:** Duetting and stitching influencers' videos are two powerful tools for getting their attention. The more creative you are, the more likely they are to drop a comment thanking you, bringing more attention to your account and video. If you're lucky, they might even duet you back to feature your content to their audience!

>> **Give:** You have many ways to give. The most straightforward, even if you have just a dollar or two, is to join one of their TikTok livestreams and purchase a virtual gift to send them. I talk more about livestreaming in Chapter 9.

Some influencers have links on their profiles to a Venmo account where you can send them donations. Some link to products and merchandise you can purchase, or a favorite charity they want to support. Some influencers create online content for a living (crazy, right?) and any monetary donation or purchase gets their attention!

>> **Support:** Seek out creative ways to support influencers. Maybe they mention a need but don't overtly ask for assistance — see if you can help them as you start to identify their needs. For example, I reached out to @catieosaurus with support by offering to feature her in this book, as shown in Figure 5-5.

FIGURE 5-5: Reaching out to @catieosaurus.

Courtesy of Catie O (@catieosaurus)

Understanding TikTok's Rules

To find accounts to feature as examples in this book, I posted a video on the @tiktokfordummiesbook account, requesting other TikTokers to share reasons why I should include them in the book. The video was an instant hit! To my surprise, though, a day or two after I posted the video, TikTok removed it for online bullying and harassment. Their moderators, I believe, thought I was calling my audience "dummies."

This sent hundreds of thousands of views and many people's responses and duets down the drain! I have to preface many of my videos now with "Disclaimer: You're NOT a dummy!"

I quickly learned from this experience that TikTok is serious about their community guidelines — the rules for their platform. One simple mistake could kill dozens of hours spent making a video — and get your account banned!

TIP

To access and read the full community guidelines, tap on Me in the bottom navigation, and then tap the three dots in the upper right. Then, scroll quite a ways down the menu until you see About, and tap Community Guidelines.

I provide the following list of TikTok's rule categories to help you avoid breaking the rules:

>> **Violent extremism:** Don't incite or threaten violence. TikTok does not allow groups that condone violence or people representing those groups.

>> **Hateful behavior:** Do not engage in hate speech of any kind, including slurs and ideologies that dehumanize individuals and groups based on race, ethnicity, national origin, religion, sexual orientation, gender, disability, and other protected attributes.

>> **Illegal activities and regulated goods:** Don't post a video that promotes physical harm or risks the safety of others. TikTok also prohibits content that depicts

- Illegal and criminal activities or teaches people how to commit crime.

- The trade of firearms and anything related to firearms.

- Gambling.

- Weaponry, even toys. TikToker @darkarcana shared with me that she had a video removed because it had a foam sword prop in the video. (She got around this by placing a censor bar over the sword.) Don't shoot me if you don't like this rule — I'm just the messenger!

- The sale, promotion, manufacture, or misuse of legal drugs or alcohol. You can talk about and use *legal* drugs and alcohol and show them in your videos.

>> **Violent and graphic content:** Violence and gore, including that of animals or humans, are not allowed.

>> **Suicide, self-harm, and dangerous acts:** Anything that encourages or promotes suicidal ideation, normalization, or glorification is prohibited. TikTok encourages users to share, in healthy ways, their experiences with these issues and how to find support. The same applies to self-harm, eating disorders, and other harmful acts to one's self.

>> **Harassment and bullying:** Users can't shame, bully, harass, or intimidate others (or even mock doing so, which is how I inadvertently got in trouble). Sexual harassment, threats, and blackmail are also not allowed.

» **Adult nudity and sexual activities:** This category includes content that might promote or glorify non-consensual sexual acts. In addition, implicit acts of a sexual nature, mentions of sexual fetishes, and sexual language are not allowed.

» **Minor safety:** TikTok takes seriously their commitment to keep kids safe on the platform. Anything illegal surrounding children and minors will be deleted and reported to authorities.

» **Integrity and authenticity:** If you're an elite hacker just aching to share the latest backdoor or robot that artificially generates views and followers, don't do it! TikTok wants real accounts and real followers on its service. Impersonation of other people, misinformation, and IP violations aren't allowed.

» **Platform security:** Don't hack, reverse-engineer, or distribute viruses on TikTok. I think most of you are outside this category, but it needs to be said.

IN THIS CHAPTER

» Controlling who sees your videos

» Adjusting your privacy settings

» Protecting your children

» Reporting, blocking, or removing
   bullies and trolls

Chapter 6

Staying Safe on TikTok

'm a dad of seven kids (you heard that right). I have two young daughters who love making TikToks with me on a regular basis, and their safety and protection is a high priority. In this chapter, I show you the powerful tools TikTok provides to help parents keep their children — and themselves — safe on the platform.

Setting Up Your Account Privacy

The first step in staying safe is to be purposeful in the target audiences for your videos. While being as public as possible can be beneficial, you might want to use TikTok simply as a way to stay in touch with close friends and family or to keep an eye on your children.

Through the privacy settings screen, TikTok enables you to set global defaults for who can see your videos. Follow these steps:

1. **Tap Me in the bottom navigation.**

   The profile page appears. If you don't see the Me icon, tap the back arrow (<) in the upper left until you see the Me icon.

2. **Tap the three dots in the upper right.**

   The Settings and Privacy screen appears.

3. **Tap Privacy.**

   The screen shown in Figure 6-1 appears.

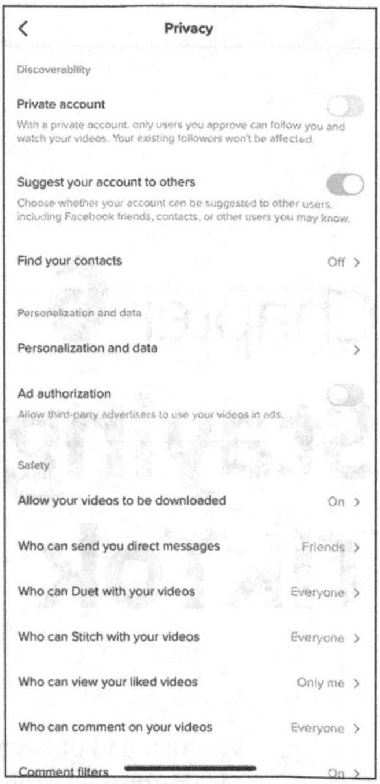

The privacy screen is your one-stop shop for all things privacy on TikTok. On this screen, you'll find the following options. (The default setting for anyone 16 and older is in parentheses — those 13–15 have more restricted privacy settings by default.)

FIGURE 6-1: Change your privacy settings here.

>> **Private Account (disabled if over 15):** When your account is listed as private, only users you add as friends can see your videos. If you list your age as 13–15, this feature is disabled by default, but you can change it to public. See more on limits for children in the next section, "Keeping Your Children Safe."

>> **Suggest Your Account to Others (enabled):** TikTok suggests your account to other TikTok users through the For You page, based on similar interests but also on your Facebook friends, phone contacts, and other friends it detects. If you don't want to be discovered by others, including friends from other services, disable this option.

>> **Find Your Contacts (Off):** Tap to turn on this setting and go to a screen where you can sync your phone contacts with TikTok.

>> **Personalization and Data:** Tap to go to a screen where you can opt into receiving personalized ads, based on your user activity. (Otherwise, you'll see only generic ads.) You can also request a copy of all your data stored on TikTok.

WARNING

It's not entirely clear when TikTok stores your activity and when they share that data with third-party advertisers. However, opting to receive personalized ads gives TikTok one more reason to share your data with third-party advertisers and marketing companies.

>> **Ad Authorization (disabled):** When enabled, third-party advertisers can use your video in their ads, which could result in more followers and a lot more attention. However, third-party advertisers would also get more of your data.

>> **Allow Your Videos to Be Downloaded (On):** This setting, the first under Safety, allows viewers to download your videos. You use this setting to determine what is selected by default before you publish. You can change this setting manually for each video individually on the publish screen (see Chapter 4).

>> **Comment Filters (On):** Skip down to this setting under Safety, and then tap it to access the comment filters screen shown in Figure 6-2. You can enable automatic filtering of any comments TikTok thinks might be spam or offensive. I suggest leaving this option On.

FIGURE 6-2:
Adding keywords on the comment filters screen.

The other option on this screen, Filter Keywords, is disabled by default. Enable this option to add a list of keywords that you don't want in your comments. Tap Add Keywords, and then type a keyword up to 30 characters. Tap Done (iPhone) or the check mark (Android) to save. You can add as many keywords as you want. When a follower types one of these keywords into the comments on any of your videos, a message appears saying the keyword is not allowed.

>> **Blocked accounts:** This option is the last one under Safety. Tap it to display a list of accounts you've blocked. You can remove accounts here as well. For details on blocking accounts, see "Dealing with Bullies and Trolls," later in the chapter.

With the exception of your liked videos (as explained shortly), the remaining settings under Safety provide three options: Everyone, Friends, or Only Me (or No One). Everyone and Only Me (or No One) are self-explanatory. Selecting Friends means only followers you follow can perform that action:

>> **Who Can Send You Direct Messages (Friends):** Gives you full control of the types of people that send you direct messages (DMs).

>> **Who Can Duet with Your Videos (Everyone):** Sets the default audience for each individual video you create. You can change this setting for each video individually on the publish screen.

>> **Who Can Stitch with Your Videos (Everyone):** Sets the default audience for each individual video you create. You can change this setting for each video individually on the publish screen.

>> **Who Can View Your Liked Videos (Only Me):** Sets the default audience for who can see the list of liked videos on your profile page. You can choose Only Me or Everyone. A list of videos you've liked appears on your profile page along with a heart icon (Everyone) or a heart icon with a not symbol (Only Me), as shown in the middle of Figure 6-3. If you select Everyone, every video you like on TikTok is listed on your profile for the public to view.

Sometimes it's helpful to allow the public to see your likes on your profile page. For instance, I allow the public to see the @tiktokfordummiesbook account's likes so I can feature people who duet or stitch videos I share on the account and point out interesting videos. If you're liking videos to show them to your audience, as in my @tiktokfordummiesbook example, setting this feature to Everyone might be advantageous.

» **Who Can Comment on Your Videos (Everyone):** Determines who can comment on each video. The settings are Everyone, Friends, and No One. If you're trying to increase your number of followers, leave this option set to Everyone. If you have other purposes for your account, consider the other options based on how private and engaging you want your account to be by default.

FIGURE 6-3:
The Liked section on your profile page.

Changing these settings does not change the audience settings for already published videos. To change the privacy on published videos, you must go to each video individually, tap the share icon, tap Privacy Settings, and make your change.

These settings are bound to change as the app adds and removes features. If your settings look different than what you see here and you have questions, ask them via the Q&A feature on the book's TikTok account at https://tiktok.com/@tiktokfor dummiesbook or the Facebook Group I created at https://facebook.com/groups/tiktokfordummies.

Keeping Your Children Safe

As a service that began with mostly minors using the app in its Musical.ly days, TikTok takes the safety of children seriously! Here are a few things TikTok does by default to keep your children safe, depending on their age range.

Protecting kids under 13

For those under 13 in the United States, TikTok offers a limited app experience called TikTok for Younger Users, which meets US privacy laws for children online. This experience is intended to let younger children gain practice in the creative spirit of TikTok while keeping them safe.

Here is what children under 13 can't and can do on TikTok:

>> They can't comment on videos they watch, direct message other users, or publish content they create.

>> They can create and save videos and explore their creativity, which is what TikTok was built for. However, the videos are not saved by TikTok and can't be viewed by others.

TikTok does not allow the sharing of personal information for anyone under 13.

TIP

As a parent, I know a preteen is going to do what a preteen is going to do! If you find that an underage child (under 13) is using TikTok, you can report the child's account to www.tiktok.com/legal/report/privacy, and TikTok will take appropriate action.

Family pairing for teens 13 to 17

The main TikTok experience is designed for those who are 13 and older. Therefore, the majority of TikTok features you read about in this book are available only for those older than 13. If you have teenagers between the ages of 13 and 17, TikTok recommends that parents enable *family pairing*, a feature that allows you to customize safety settings to suit your comfort level.

Do the following to enable the family pairing feature:

1. **On the parent's profile, tap Me in the bottom navigation.**

2. **Tap the three dots in the upper right of the profile page.**

3. **On the Settings and Privacy screen, under Content and Activity, tap Family Pairing.**

   If this is your first time adding a child, the screen shown in Figure 6-4, left, appears. Otherwise, it looks like the screen on the right.

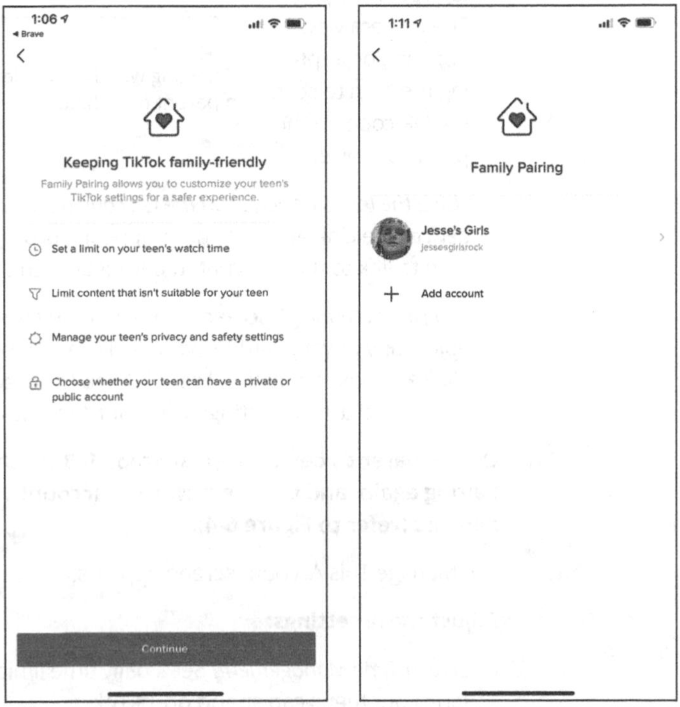

FIGURE 6-4: Introducing the family pairing feature.

4. **Do one of the following:**

   - *If this is your first time adding a child:* Tap Continue. On the next screen, tap the Parent option, as shown in Figure 6-5.

   - *If you have previously followed these steps for a child:* Tap Add Account.

A QR code appears on the screen. Leave this screen open on your device.

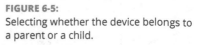

5. **On the teen's device, do the following:**

   a. *Open his or her account.* Or ask your teen to do it.

   b. *Follow Steps 1–4 but tap Teen in Step 4.* The camera view appears, prompting the teen to scan the QR code on the parent's device.

FIGURE 6-5:
Selecting whether the device belongs to a parent or a child.

   c. *Using the teen's device, scan the QR code on the parent's device.* The Link Accounts page appears, prompting the teen to link to the designated parent account.

   d. *Tap Link Accounts.* A screen appears, letting the teen adjust any privacy settings you've allowed to be changed. TikTok chooses a minimal set of defaults based on age. You can adjust the settings you want to allow in Step 7.

6. **On the parent's device, repeat Steps 1–3 to load Family Pairing again, and tap the new teen account that appears (refer to Figure 6-4).**

   The Manage This Account screen appears.

7. **Adjust these settings:**

   - *Screen Time Management:* Set a daily time limit for how long your teens can spend on TikTok.

   - *Restricted Mode:* Restrict content not suitable for all audiences.

WARNING

   I don't know if it's a feature or a bug, but if you switch from your parent account to a child's account (on the same device) with restricted mode enabled, you can't switch back to your parent account! You must delete TikTok from your device and reinstall it to log back into your parent account.

- *Search:* Disable the Discover Search bar, which means teens won't be able to search for specific content.

- *Privacy and Safety:* Override some of the privacy settings described in "Setting Up Your Account Privacy," earlier in this chapter. You can set your teen's account to a private account; turn off suggesting your teen's account to others; and adjust who can send direct messages to your teen, see your teen's liked videos, and comment on your teen's videos.

As the parent, you can decide how much freedom and privacy to give your teens. This approach at least lets you ensure their safety. You may also want to follow their account, even if privately, so you can see what they're posting online.

TIP

For detailed instructions on how to protect your children on Tik-Tok, check out the For Parents: Safety Center at www.tiktok.com/safety/resources/for-parents.

Dealing with Bullies and Trolls

You use TikTok to have fun while finding creative ways to share content. Unfortunately, you'll likely encounter some people who take away that fun. Don't worry. TikTok makes it easy to deal with bullies and trolls.

You can delete comments on any TikTok video you create but not on other creators' videos. To delete a comment on a TikTok video you create, hold down on the comment and tap Delete. Or add comment filters on your privacy settings screen, mentioned earlier in this chapter, to automatically remove comments that keep appearing with certain keywords.

Sometimes an "out of sight, out of mind" approach works with bullies and trolls. You can remove, block, and report followers. To perform these actions, tap the person's username or profile picture to get to the person's profile page. Then tap the three dots in the upper right to display the Send To dialog, shown in Figure 6-6. Note the following options:

>> **Report:** If the problematic user is doing anything that violates the TikTok terms (for example, bullying), tap Report and follow the instructions.

>> **Block:** If the bully or troll keeps coming back, you'll want to block the person so he or she not only can't see your account but also can't comment or interact with you. Tap Block and confirm the blocking.

>> **Remove This Follower:** Remove a follower so he or she can no longer follow you. (You'll continue to follow the person if you were doing so previously). Removing yourself from a person's Following page might make the person forget about you and move on.

FIGURE 6-6:
The Send
To dialog
on a user's
profile
page.

In the end, if any form of bullying or trolling gets to be too much, you can adjust your privacy settings. For example, in a particularly controversial video, you could turn off comments to prevent too much argument and trolling. You have control over how much interaction you want with any given user or users.

Building Your TikTok Following

Analyze your TikTok account data.

Discover the tips influencers use to create videos that go viral.

Share your videos interactively through duetting and stitching.

Chapter **7**

Looking at Your Profile Stats

Today's culture seems far different from the culture I grew up with. My children and their friends seem to be obsessed with how many followers and views they have on social media, almost as a form of identity. Although it's probably not healthy to base one's identity on an online popularity contest, growing followers and video views on TikTok does have value. This chapter shows parents and their kids a more productive way to funnel their desire for followers.

Understanding the Value of Followers

Gaining followers on TikTok can be valuable for several reasons, among them the following:

» **You own a business and need to satisfy business goals.**
Social media is a prime landscape for building a large,

passionate customer base that engages with your products and drives sales for your business. The larger and more specific follower base you can build, the more sales you're capable of generating. I talk about using TikTok for business in Part 3.

TIP

If you ask me a question publicly via the Q&A feature on my profile (@jessestay) or the @tiktokfordummies account, I try to answer for free as much as I can. If I can't answer immediately, you can ask others on the book's Facebook group (https://facebook.com/groups/tiktokfordummies), and sometimes I respond there as well. Otherwise, I am always happy to find a consulting package that you can afford, which is how I pay the bills (shameless plug).

>> **You want to attract sponsors and earn money for your content.** As an influencer on TikTok and other platforms, I regularly have businesses approach me, asking if they can sponsor me to post content on their behalf. As you gain more followers, you could make the case for content sponsorship.

When you have 10,000+ followers on TikTok, you can apply for the Creator Fund program, which automatically pays you based on the number of views your videos get. It's not much, but as you gain more followers, the amount you're paid grows substantially!

Note: You need a Creator account (free) to be eligible for the Creator Fund program. To make the switch, tap the following: the Me icon, the three dots in the upper right, Manage Account, and finally Switch to Creator Account. Answer the questions presented and — voila! — you're in.

>> **You have a message you want the world to hear.** If you have a cause you want to promote or a message you're passionate about the world hearing, building your follower base gives you a much larger audience for your message.

>> **You want leverage to connect with more influential people in your career.** Growing my own follower base and being strategic with online connections has been fundamental to meeting some of the most influential people in the world, even Facebook's Mark Zuckerberg! I strongly recommend using your follower growth strategy in a way that builds your business and career network. Follow my advice in Chapter 5 to gain the attention of and build rapport with TikTok influencers.

>> **You want to livestream to your audience.** Livestreaming is the biggest reason to initially try to grow followers. TikTok doesn't allow you to livestream until you have 1,000+ followers. See Chapter 5 for details on engaging as much as you can with other TikTokers, and you'll hit this number in no time. I talk more about livestreaming in Chapter 9.

That's my list of reasons. Feel free to suggest your own ideas and tag me on this book's account at `https://tiktok.com/@tiktokfordummiesbook`.

Breaking Down Your Following, Followers, Likes, and Views

After you determine why you want to increase your TikTok audience, how do you know you're getting results? Figure 7-1 shows various metrics you can track to see if you're moving toward achieving your TikTok growth goals.

Following are the numbers you see on your profile page (which you access by tapping Me in the bottom navigation), no matter what kind of account you have (Business or Creator not required):

>> **Following:** The number of people you're following on TikTok. Tap the Following count on your profile page to see a list of everyone you're following.

FIGURE 7-1:
Checking the numbers on your Profile page.

>> **Followers:** The number of people following your videos on TikTok. Tap the number to see a list of who's following the account.

>> **Likes:** The number of likes on all your videos combined. This number is a good indication of whether your videos are getting people to take action of some sort.

>> **Views:** The number of times a particular video was viewed. Typically, the more views your videos receive, the more followers you can gain. This number appears in the lower-left corner of each video listed on your profile page.

Looking at Detailed Account Analytics

TikTok provides more detailed numbers for your account via the Analytics tool, which is under Creator on the Settings and Privacy screen.

REMEMBER

You won't see the Creator option and subsequently your account analytics unless you have a Business or Creator account. Switching to a Business or Creator account takes only minutes and it's free. Tap Me, the three dots icon, Manage Account, and then Switch to Business Account. Answer the questions (only a few), and you're done. It's that easy.

In Chapter 11, I show you how to use the Analytics tool for business. For now, follow these steps to access your account's analytics:

1. **Tap Me in the bottom navigation.**

   Your profile page appears. If you don't see the Me icon, tap the back arrow (<) in the upper left until the icon appears.

2. **Tap the three dots in the upper right.**

3. **On the Settings and Privacy screen, tap Creator Tools.**

4. **On the Creator screen, tap Analytics.**

The Analytics screen appears, as shown in Figure 7-2, with a detailed overview of your video views, followers, and profile views. The tabs at the top provide more detail about your content, followers, and livestreams.

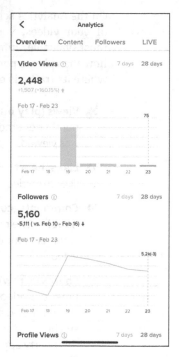

In the preceding section, I describe your profile page's cumulative statistics about your total number of followers, viewers, and likes. You can also find out about the performance of an individual video. If you have a Business or Creator account, follow these steps to access individual video analytics:

FIGURE 7-2:
The Analytics screen.

1. **Tap Me in the bottom navigation.**

If you don't see the Me icon, tap the back arrow (<) in the upper left until it appears.

2. **On your profile page, tap one of your videos.**

The selected video loads, playing on repeat.

3. **Tap the three dots on the right, below the comments icon.**

4. **In the More dialog that appears, tap Analytics.**

The Analytics screen appears with all the data TikTok collected for your selected video, as shown in Figure 7-3. A video I made of my adorable daughter brushing her hair went viral in 2020.

On the Analytics screen for each of your videos, you'll find the most valuable information on how the video is performing and where its traffic is coming from:

>> **Views (play button):** The number of times the video was viewed.

>> **Likes (heart):** How many likes the video received.

>> **Comments (comment bubble):** The number of comments for the selected video.

>> **Shares (arrow):** How many times the video has been shared, including duets, stitches, and shares to third-party apps through TikTok.

>> **Total Play Time:** How long users collectively spent watching the video. As you can see in Figure 7-3, 1.3 million views equals a lot of time spent on TikTok (in this case, just watching my cute daughter brush her hair for 15 seconds)!

>> **Average Watch Time:** How long, on average, users spend watching the video before swiping up to the next video.

TIP

If the average watch time is shorter than the video length, your audience wasn't captivated for the entire video's length. TikTok's algorithm favors videos that have longer average watch times, which is why I try to stick to creating 15 second (or shorter) videos.

>> **Traffic Source Types:** Where viewers are finding your videos. In Figure 7-3, most of the video traffic came from the For You page. This generally means most traffic is from new users who weren't following my account when they first saw the video. From this metric, I can look at my total

FIGURE 7-3:
The Analytics screen for an individual video.

new followers for the past day or week (see Chapter 11), evaluate if I'm getting many new followers from these new viewers, and try to understand why or why not.

If the numbers are significant enough, TikTok also shows other traffic source statistics in this section, showing viewers who discovered the selected video

- Through your personal profile.

- By following your account.

- From a list of videos that used the same sound you used. (To see this list, tap Discover in the bottom navigation and then search for the name of the sound that scrolls across the bottom of your video. Or go click the sound icon in the bottom right of the video.)

- By discovering your video through a search query.

- From a list of videos that appeared by searching for a hashtag you used in your description.

» **Reached Audience:** The number of users who saw your video, which is not the same as the number of views. Some users might watch a video multiple times, as was the case with the video in Figure 7-3.

» **Audience Territories:** A list of where your viewers are located around the world. This list could help you decide, for example, whether to add other languages to your videos to accommodate an international audience.

TIP

Your analytics give you clues on what is and isn't working in your videos. Refer often to all the numbers I mention in this chapter to get ideas on how to improve your videos. When a particular video garners a lot of views and gets you more followers, study that video to see which of its elements you can repeat in other videos, so you can continue to get more views, engagement, and followers.

For a more detailed analysis of your account's analytics, especially if you use TikTok for your business, see Chapter 11, where I show you how to take your TikTok numbers to the next level.

Chapter 8

Creating Viral Content

As you read this book, I bet you're asking one of the top questions I get from my audiences, "How can I become TikTok famous?" *TikTok famous* is a term commonly used in the community to mean someone with a lot of followers. In Chapter 7, I discuss the reasons why growing your followers can be a benefit to you. In this chapter, I show you how to grow those followers through engaging content.

Understanding the TikTok Algorithm

Knowing a little about the TikTok algorithm can help you better understand what makes a video go viral. An *algorithm* is a calculation that search engines and social media platforms use to rank content — in the case of TikTok, to rank videos and customize For You page results. It's basically the "secret sauce" of how TikTok decides what videos to show each user. If you understand the basics of TikTok's algorithm, you can understand how to create content that shows up more often on the For You pages of people who don't follow you. Knowing this secret sauce gives you the ability to gain more followers and views.

WARNING

A disclaimer: The actual TikTok algorithm — the inner workings of how TikTok surfaces content on the For You page — is a secret. It also changes frequently, and what might work today may not work tomorrow, so test your content often. That said, I and other creators have discovered basic principles that seem to result in more followers and views. The tips I share here are based on what I've found to be effective.

Here are a few principles to remember as you create videos. These could help make your videos more likely to show up on the For You page:

>> **Content is king, but engagement is queen and wears the pants.** Focus on engagement first. A video that moves its audience to take action — like, comment, duet, or stitch — will see *far* greater views and new followers than a well-produced video that took hours to create. I have almost 15 years' experience creating content for social media — trust me, this is true!

TIP

You want your audience to feel something quickly — within the first five seconds of your video, if you can manage it. They hear a voice saying, "I just have to say something!" and then leave a comment, create a stitch, or duet your video. Success!

TikTok and most social media platforms favor lots of engagement on videos, especially when users are willing to take the time to have a conversation. This is why even controversial content tends to see more views.

>> **Don't forget to make your content king.** A well-produced, well-lit video with good sound and good editing gains some level of favor in the TikTok algorithm. I share tips for improving content quality later in the chapter.

>> **Look to your royal subjects to understand what's trending.** You probably discovered TikTok because someone close to you — a child, niece, nephew, or friend — shared a funny video. These days, a lot of Internet trends begin on TikTok. Much of TikTok culture centers around one large, connected community, all talking about the same things. The TikTok algorithm highly favors content that remains a part of this "town gossip."

BUSINESSES FOLLOW THE GOSSIP, TOO

Knowing what memes, hashtags, sounds, and trends are popular at the moment is critical to knowing how to make content go viral on TikTok. Successful business accounts take this into consideration for their TikTok content strategy. Accounts such as the *Washington Post,* Taco Bell, and Dunkin' don't just post their regular social media content on TikTok. Instead, they create content that includes trending themes and memes. For example, in the figure, @tacobell uses the Time Warp effect to show off some of their popular drinks. Even the town merchants get in on the town gossip!

Want to double your video views? Find a popular TikTok influencer who's participating in a popular trend, and duet or stitch that person's content with your own twist on the conversation. Even if the creator doesn't notice you, TikTok's algorithm tends to favor videos that duet or stitch the videos of popular creators. When I do this in my videos, such as the one in Figure 8-1, I always see significantly more views, especially when I'm creative with my response.

>> **Attention spans are short! Focus your content.** Although engagement trumps content and length, TikTok's For You page algorithm tends to favor content that is short. People on TikTok have short attention spans. In addition, TikTok favors videos where most of the viewers watch the entire video. Unless I'm doing something to engage my audience, such as a duet or stitch, I keep my content shorter than 15 seconds. This makes it more likely that my viewers will watch the entire video, giving an added bump to the video's chances of being seen on the For You page of potential followers.

FIGURE 8-1:
Duetting my popular videos on @tiktokfordummies generates more views because that account has more followers.

Because TikTok gives a boost to videos that get more viewers to watch to the end, consider splitting a long video into segments. Make sure each segment starts with a new hook to keep the viewer interested.

Watch your numbers! TikTok is constantly changing, and what works for me and other accounts on TikTok today might work differently for you later. See Chapters 7 and 11 for more about which numbers to track (likes, followers, and so on).

>> **Time your messages carefully.** When you post a video, TikTok looks at the video's content, description, hashtags, sounds, and other details, and determines its ideal audience. First TikTok shares the video with a small, targeted audience. If they respond well, it increases the audience — and continues to do so as long as viewers react favorably. However, TikTok's algorithm needs time to get your video to that full audience.

If you post a new video targeting the same audience as the last-published video too quickly, it confuses the algorithm. Your original video will not be able to make it to as many people as it could have. I've found no established guide-lines on how soon is too soon to post, but pay attention to this issue as you publish videos and see what works best.

You can upload a video to be posted later. See Chapter 4 for details.

>> **Consistency is your key to the kingdom.** If you haven't done so already, think about what you want your TikTok account to be about. What goals do you want to accomplish with it? What topics do you want to focus on? Who's your target audience? Take some time to answer those questions. I discuss researching your audience in Chapter 10, mostly for people with business goals that they want to accomplish on TikTok, but the info is useful and applies to everyone.

Next, make sure every video you create matches the answers to those questions. If you keep all your content consistent, TikTok knows immediately what audiences to send your content to, and you're more likely to see higher growth more quickly. Maintaining consistency is keeping a promise to your audience: They come to you looking for specific content, and you deliver it.

Identifying Trending Content

A great way to gain followers and increase video views on TikTok is by understanding what content is trending. In this section, I discuss finding trends by browsing the discover page and using the search function.

Checking the discover page

To access the discover page, shown in Figure 8-2, tap Discover in the main navigation. Scroll through the main discover page to see what's currently trending, and then tap the Sounds and Hashtags tabs to explore those pages further and get new inspiration.

Swipe the top banner to see trending accounts, sounds, themes, and hashtags. These are things TikTok wants you to see, so TikTok will favor your videos on the For You page if you use them in your content.

Tap a topic on the banner to see a screen with that topic, such as the #CarTikTok page shown in Figure 8-3, left, which includes videos, sounds, hashtags, and a list of the top-viewed videos

FIGURE 8-2:
The discover page.

using the topic. Sometimes topic pages are just a landing page TikTok has designed with a partner or an advertiser, such as the Song Breaker Awards sponsored by @logitec, as shown in Figure 8-3, right.

FIGURE 8-3:
The
#CarTikTok
(left) and
@logitec
Song
Breaker
Awards
(right)
topic
pages.

Each topic page will be different, designed to show off the things TikTok wants its users to consider in their videos. Explore these videos, sounds, or hashtags on each topic page and look for common themes or elements, such as a dance, a song, or an activity. If the topic you're exploring contains a trending hashtag, consider adding it to your description. Or you could create a video matching what each video is discussing but in your own way. Tap the back icon (<) to return to the discover page.

Scroll down the discover page to see what's hot. Tap a video or two to see any common themes, and consider integrating those elements into your own videos. Tap a sound or hashtag to see a list of videos using that sound or hashtag.

When you tap a trending sound, you can tap the Use This Sound button (see Figure 8-4, left) to immediately start recording a video using that sound. If you tap a trending hashtag, tap the record button (see Figure 8-4, right), and any effects, sounds, and other elements associated with that hashtag automatically load into a new recording screen for you, as shown in Figure 8-5.

FIGURE 8-4: You can use trending sounds and hashtags easily in your own videos.

I typically sift through all the elements on the discover page briefly before publishing a video to be sure I'm using the latest and greatest hashtags, sounds, and themes. That way, I'm more likely to see additional views.

The discover page changes constantly. The layout I discuss in this chapter may change by the time you read this. However, the principles of exploring the trending sounds, hashtags, and topics remain the same.

Finding content through search

The discover page sports a search box at the top, which you can use to find content using topics you're interested in, as well as hashtags, other users, and sounds. To search for something, go to the discover page and follow these steps:

1. **Tap the search field.**

   A list appears showing your recent searches. If this is your first time searching, the list will be empty.

2. **Type what you want to search for and then tap the Search button that appears on your device's keyboard.**

   You can enter a hashtag, name, username, song name, name of an effect, or keyword. The screen shown in Figure 8-6 appears, displaying the default Top tab, with results organized by the top videos, hashtags, and users that TikTok determines are the most relevant to your search.

FIGURE 8-5:
A themed recording screen with loaded elements.

3. **Tap a video to watch it.**

   Check out the Top tab if you're trying to get inspiration for videos on a particular topic. If you tap the Sounds or Hashtags tab, you see a screen similar to the one in the preceding section (refer to Figure 8-4).

4. **Tap another tab (Users, Videos, Sounds, or Hashtags) to see a new search view, organized for that category.**

   The categories are self-explanatory — no surprises here!

5. **To return to the discover page, tap the back icon (<) in the upper-left corner.**

FIGURE 8-6:
The search results page.

TIP

You can find trending videos, memes, sounds, and hashtags on your For You and Following pages. What catches your attention? When I see videos on either page that spark a fun idea, I mark them as favorites, so I can sift through them later. To mark a video as a favorite, long-press the video and tap Add to Favorites.

Grabbing Your Viewers' Attention

With an understanding of the TikTok algorithm and a knowledge of the type of content that's trending, you're ready to start creating videos that engage your audience! Here are a few ideas, some from a few of my favorite popular TikTokers, that are sure to get your audience talking.

Stay positive

TikTok user Aaron Hanania, shown in Figure 8-7, built an audience of tens of thousands by maintaining a message of positivity for his audience. In a message to me, he wrote:

Positivity has allowed me to grow on TikTok because it's unique to me. There are very few other influencers who not only spread positivity, but truly engage and get to know their audience. When someone joins my TikTok Live, I recognize their names; I remember things they share. And I think that's important.

You can follow Aaron at `https://tiktok.com/@aaron hanania`. Tell him I sent you!

Courtesy of Aaron Hanania (@aaronhanania)

FIGURE 8-7:
Aaron Hanania focuses on positivity.

Keep your content clean

As I mention in Chapter 6, certain types of content will get your content deleted or your account banned. Depictions of nudity, sexual content (even implied), firearms, and other forbidden topics outlined in TikTok's community guidelines are not allowed.

Know your audience. Although TikTok is full of risqué content, I've found that content that skirts the community guidelines (containing swear words and drug references) or is generally PG-13 (or above) tends to get fewer viewers. Exceptions to this rule exist, and you'll have a better response if your audience expects this type of content. However, I recommend playing it safe when you can.

STORY TIME!

My most popular video on TikTok (see the figures) received two million+ views and many followers and is still growing. All because I recorded my 5-year-old brushing her hair while she counted brush-strokes. The text on the video reads, "I told her princesses brush their hair 100 times a day." The comment section is filled with remarks ranging from, "My mom (or dad) told me that too!" to "This will for sure cause her hair to fall out!" I'm sure it's invoking an emotion in you, too, as you read this!

Although you can invoke emotion, as I discuss next, or incite controversy, you may reach a larger audience by avoiding offense in the first place. As always, test to see what works best. No judgement here — I'm all about the data and what shows results!

TIP

Some creators edit out curse words in descriptions, captions, and the text on their videos but still curse *in* the videos. If this is your desired type of content and your audience will respond well, consider this approach. TikTok's algorithm tends to give greater weight to onscreen text than audio.

Invoke emotion

Emotion — whether it's positive or negative, and whether you are showing humor, anger, sadness, or something else — makes people want to respond. When people *feel* something during a video, they want to do something with that feeling. Your goal in each video should be to invoke emotion in your audience.

That's why positivity is so important: It creates an emotion, in this case something positive or happy in the mind of the viewer. And that emotion makes them to want to do something with that feeling, such as share your video. However, controversy can also invoke emotion. TikTok users are highly opinionated, and everyone wants to share theirs!

Use a ring light and microphone

I've never seen TikTok officially say this, but it seems to me and other experts that TikTok favors videos in which faces are clearly visible and voices are easily heard.

The best way to improve the lighting on your face is by using a ring light. The 10-inch ring light I use costs $13 on Amazon (https://amzn.to/3r2dpJ8) and works perfectly, especially when attached to a tripod. It comes with a wireless remote and multiple brightness settings.

For a microphone, you can invest in an expensive USB processor and professional audio equipment that connects to your phone. Or just use earbuds with an attached microphone. I've seen professional musicians and voiceover actors on TikTok use just the mic on their earbuds. And the microphone I attached to my stock iPhone earbuds often gives serious competition to even the best condenser microphones on the market.

Clarify and organize your message

My friend and TikTok influencer, Elisha Lee (https://tiktok.com/@goodtoknowelisha), has excellent advice on her channel. Elisha talks about how she keeps her messages organized, clear, and constrained to the 60 seconds or less time limit that TikTok allows. In her video on this topic (see Figure 8-8), she recommends that you

1. Start with a paragraph of what you want to say.
2. Reduce that paragraph down to as FEW words as possible!!!

She then suggests that you memorize the paragraph, and then recite it from memory in short bursts, with each burst representing a clip in your recording. This process ensures that your message is crisp and fully vetted, includes only what

Courtesy of Elisha Lee (@goodtoknowelisha)

FIGURE 8-8:
@goodtoknowelisha shows how to keep videos clear and organized.

you want your audience to hear, and will fit in the time constraint of your video.

Consider third-party tools

TikTok is the "movie studio in your pocket" that I mention throughout this book. However, it doesn't have everything you might need to add that creative edge to your videos. Here are apps I like to use on my iPhone:

>> **The native Photos app:** Many TikTokers like to use widely available video editing apps, but my phone's native Photos app gives me everything I need to trim, crop, rotate, and even apply filters to videos I want to upload to TikTok.

>> **Reface:** Reface allows you to upload a selfie and morph that person's face onto another photo or animated GIF. Just make sure you have the permission of anyone whose likeness you include. I keep Reface in my toolkit because it enables me to add morph effects, which is something other creators don't use much. The Reface app has helped me create fun and sometimes hilarious videos as a result.

TIP

Search for *effects* in your device's app store to find apps that you can use to add other types of special effects that might give your videos an edge.

>> **GIF Maker:** This app allows you to make animated GIFs from your videos. After making an animated GIF, I like to import it into Reface (see preceding bullet), morph my face onto another's (or vice versa), and export the GIF as a video. I can then apply audio with a movie editor (such as iMovie).

>> **MP3 Converter:** This app allows me to extract the audio from a video on my phone for later use. I select the video, tap Export, and save the audio as an MP3 file on my phone. I can then add the file to another video using a movie editor app such iMovie.

>> **SaveTok:** When you save a video from TikTok to your device, the beginning and end of the video are usually superimposed with the TikTok logo and your username. The SaveTok app downloads a copy of your video from TikTok to your device without the superimposed TikTok logo and username. I like to use the SaveTok app to upload my own videos recorded outside TikTok as duets and stitches. To learn how to do this, see the "Duetting and stitching with prerecorded video" sidebar.

>> **Captions for TikTok:** Many people don't use TikTok with the sound on. Placing captions in your videos allows you to share your message without sound. The Captions app converts what you're saying to text, and then displays the text in a pretty format inside your video. You can save the new video to your device and upload it to TikTok later.

>> **iMovie or another movie editor:** Having a good movie editor on your phone gives you the ability to combine video with new audio, merge videos, crop videos, and put videos side by side. Some video editors have additional effects that can be applied before you upload the video to TikTok.

DUETTING AND STITCHING WITH PRERECORDED VIDEO

TikTok doesn't allow you to upload your own videos as duets or stitches. You can only use TikTok's native record functionality to duet or stitch someone. To get around this, I use the following hack:

1. **In TikTok, copy the URL of the video you want to duet or stitch by tapping Send To and then Copy.**

2. **Open the SaveTok app and tap the Save TikTok button at the bottom of the home screen to paste the video's URL from Step 1. Then tap the Save Now button at the bottom of the video screen to save the video to your device.**

   The video is downloaded to your device's photo storage.

3. **Record and edit the video that you plan to add as a duet or stitch to the video you downloaded in Step 2.**

4. **Edit your duet or stitch in your video editor of choice.**

   For a duet, place your own video from Step 3 next to the video you downloaded in Step 2, so it looks like a TikTok duet would look. For a stitch, add your video from Step 3 to the end of the video you downloaded in Step 1. Make sure you stay under the 60-second maximum time limit for both videos, combined.

5. **Save the final video to your device's photo storage, and upload it to TikTok.**

6. **Select the combined video you just created, and add any sounds, effects, or additional pizazz you think it needs. Then proceed through editing the video (see Chapter 4), and tap Next when done to get to the Publish screen.**

   Your video now looks like a normal TikTok duet or stitch.

7. **On the final publish screen, in your description, type #duet with @*username* or #stitch with @*username*, replacing @*username* with the username of the TikTok user you are dueting or stitching with.**

   See Chapter 4 for details. You can include additional text after @*username* if you want.

8. Tap Publish when everything looks right.

Your duet or stitch is published to your followers. And because the person you're duetting with is mentioned in the description, she will see it as a mention in her inbox notifications.

Note that in this approach, if followers tap *@username,* they go to the user's profile page rather than directly to the original video that you duetted or stitched. This approach is a bit of a hack, but it's a fun way to get the job done when I need to do things in my duets and stitches that TikTok can't!

There you have it. The cat is out of the bag. These are all my secrets for creating viral content. As you use these tips and discover new approaches to going viral, be sure to tag @tiktokfordummiesbook with your own tips!

Chapter **9**

Reaching New Audiences with Advanced Features

TikTok has some pretty cool features that can help you reach more people and grow your followers. These features — duet, stitch, and live — are a little more advanced, which is why I saved them for this chapter. If you use these features consistently in fun and creative ways, I think you can increase your followers by reaching audiences you haven't interacted with before on TikTok.

Duetting with Your Favorite Videos

Duetting, as TikTok calls it, is one of my favorite ways to share videos on TikTok. You can create your own videos that play alongside any other video that has the duet feature enabled. The capability to duet side-by-side with other creators makes TikTok a much more connected and friendly environment than other social networking environments, as you'll quickly discover.

To duet a video on TikTok, first go to the video. Then as it plays, follow these steps:

1. **Tap the share icon (right-pointing arrow).**

2. **In the Send To dialog that appears, tap the Duet icon.**

   Voila! A recording screen appears, as shown in Figure 9-1. Refer to Chapter 3 if you need a refresher on recording videos.

REMEMBER

   If the Duet icon appears dimmed, the creator has disabled the duet feature before publishing the video.

REMEMBER

   By default, duets record with the microphone of your device turned off, meaning viewers of your newly created duet will hear only the video you're watching. To include sound in your recording, tap the Mic icon.

FIGURE 9-1:
The recording screen for a duet, with a side-by-side layout.

3. **(Optional) If you want to change the layout, tap the Layout icon and select a layout. Tap outside the menu when you're finished.**

   The Layout menu appears, as shown in Figure 9-2, listing the layout options for duetting:

   - *Left & Right:* The video you're recording is on the left and the original video is on the right.

   - *React:* The original video appears in a small rectangle inside the video you're recording.

   - *Top & Bottom:* The video you're recording is on the top and the original video is on the bottom.

   - *3 Screens:* Your video appears in the center, with the original video appearing both above and below it.

   If you're using Left & Right or Top & Bottom, you can tap the Switch icon (above and to the right of the layout options) to swap places between what you're recording and the original video.

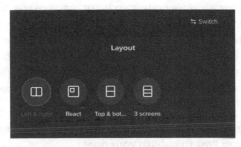

FIGURE 9-2:
Your
layout
options.

4. **(Optional) Add effects and filters, and start and stop the recording to create clips.**

   The rest of the process is just like a normal recording. For details on what you can do and how to do it, see Chapter 3.

5. **Start recording using the quick-tap or tap-and-hold method.**

   The recording begins (see Figure 9-3), and the video you've chosen to duet plays alongside what you're recording, allowing you to react to and participate with the video in real time.

You can also use the timer feature, mentioned in Chapter 3, to start a duet or stitch.

6. **Tap the red check mark when you're finished recording all clips of your duetted video.**

If you exhaust your time limit, TikTok will automatically take you to the Edit screen in the next step.

FIGURE 9-3: Recording during a duet.

7. **Edit the video to your liking, and then tap Next.**

See Chapter 4 for details regarding editing.

Ensuring that your voice is clear and audible in a duet will help your audience understand your message over the person you're duetting. Adjust the volume, as shown in Chapter 4, so that your voice (called the *added sound* in a duet) is loud enough to be heard over the person you're duetting. I typically increase the added sound of my voice and decrease the volume of the original sound of the person I'm duetting.

8. **Prepare the video for publishing on the post screen, and then tap Post to publish your duet.**

Again, see Chapter 4 for information on publishing your video. The screen returns to the video you just duetted, and your newly recorded duet video uploads to TikTok. After the duet has finished uploading, it plays automatically if you're on the Home screen. Otherwise, you can view it on your profile page by tapping the Me icon at the bottom of your screen.

On the post screen, note that the options to allow others to duet and stitch your duetted video. If you leave these on, others can duet or stitch your own duets and stitches, over and over — this can result in some fun group video ensembles, all playing at once with the original recorded video you just duetted!

Stitching the End of a Video

You can also *stitch*, or add, your own recording to the end of any video on TikTok, if the creator has enabled the feature. Stitching is another great way to reach audiences that you might not reach otherwise. When you stitch, you can use up to five seconds of the other video.

As you're watching the video, follow these steps to stitch your video:

1. **Tap the Share icon.**

2. **In the Send To dialog that opens, tap the Stitch icon.**

   A screen appears, as shown in Figure 9-4, with the video and a slider, where you can choose up to 5 seconds of the video you want to display before your new recording. The red box represents the part of the video you're sharing that will appear before your recording, but you can change that in the next step.

FIGURE 9-4: Selecting up to 5 seconds of the video to stitch before your recording.

3. **Drag right and left in the red box to select the portion of video you want to play in your new recording.**

   To adjust the clip's length, drag either side of the red box.

   The main video moves to the location you select in the slider box, playing on repeat for the selected length. You can pause and play the main video any time by tapping it.

4. **Tap Next in the upper-right corner.**

   The recording screen appears. The portion of the video you selected for stitching is stored as a clip at the beginning of your recording. You can record up to the 15 or 60 seconds you select, minus the length of your selected stitch.

   If you change your mind about stitching, tap X in the upper right. Then save or discard the video (if given the option).

5. **Record your remaining video, selecting either 15 or 60 seconds for your maximum length.**

   See Chapter 3 for details on recording the video.

6. **Edit and publish your stitched video.**

   For information on editing and publishing videos, see Chapter 4. The video you chose to stitch appears. When your stitched video has uploaded to TikTok, it plays automatically if you're on the Home page. Otherwise, you can view it on your profile page by tapping the Me icon at the bottom of your screen.

TIP

Stitches give you a fun opportunity to continue the action in the video you chose to stitch. For example, if someone is swinging a baseball bat in the 5 seconds you've chosen for stitching, your new recording could start with a ball moving from where the baseball bat was swinging in the original.

Livestreaming When You're TikTok Famous

When you have at least 1,000 followers and are over 16 years old, TikTok enables the livestream feature so that you can broadcast live, even to audiences who aren't following you. This feature is a great way to get more visibility and even make a little money through gifts your followers purchase. For details, see the "Live Gifting" sidebar. Note that you must be over 18 years old to send or receive gifts during a livestream.

LIVE GIFTING

Users can send their livestream host a virtual gift purchased through TikTok. When viewing a livestream, tap the gift icon in the bottom right. A menu appears with different gift options worth increasing amounts. You send a gift by using coins, which you purchase through TikTok. Note that you must be over 18 to buy them.

During livestreams, the host earns diamonds based on the number of gifts given by livestream viewers, how many viewers watched the livestream, and other factors. TikTok doesn't share the exact formula for what earns diamonds, but gifts seem to be a big part of it. As a host, you can access and cash out your diamonds by tapping Balance on the Settings and Privacy page. The gifts given by viewers during a livestream are a small token of appreciation that your viewers can send for making them feel a part of your community.

To start your first TikTok livestream, do the following:

FIGURE 9-5:
The livestream setup screen.

1. **Tap the plus sign (+) in the bottom navigation, as though you're recording a new video.**

   The recording screen appears with the Live option (if you have this feature).

2. **Tap Live.**

3. **In the livestream setup screen that appears (see Figure 9-5), add a title.**

   The title (32 or fewer characters) will appear to your followers and new potential followers to entice them to watch.

4. **Play with the icons on the right to set up your video:**

- *Flip:* Flip the camera view to the opposite camera on your device, just like on the recording screen. You can also tap anywhere on the screen to flip the view.

- *Enhance:* Apply filters to adjust the look of your face and eyes and add color overlays to the video or make it black and white.

- *Effects:* Add effects. Note that only a limited number of effects are available for livestreams.

- *Share:* Open the Send To menu, where you can notify other TikTokers, share a link to other social networks, or send a text message. To get more viewers, consider sharing with people who already know you.

You might not have many viewers of your first TikTok livestream. Be patient and keep doing livestreams even if no one watches at first.

- *Settings:* Open the menu shown in Figure 9-6, where you can turn off live gifts, turn off comments in your livestream, and set filters for what people can say in the comments. Tap Keyword Filter(0/50) to enter keywords; users are unable to comment if they mention those keywords. Tap above the menu to close it.

FIGURE 9-6:
The settings menu for livestreams.

TIP

5. **Review your video to be sure it's ready, and then tap Go Live.**

   Your livestream begins. TikTok begins notifying followers and others that you're live, and you'll see people join at the bottom, as shown in Figure 9-7.

See questions   View more options

FIGURE 9-7:
A TikTok
livestream.   Share with other platforms   End livestream

Add effects

During your livestream, people who discover your video will interact with you and you can interact with them. At the bottom of the livestream are icons you can use to view questions, tell other platforms that you're livestreaming, add effects, end the livestream, and more. You can even specify a charity, and your viewers can donate to that charity during your livestream.

Enjoy this time with your audience. This is their opportunity to get to know you and vice versa. You're building community with your followers so that they come back again and again!

6. **To end your livestream, tap the power icon in the lower right (next to the three dots).**

The live summary page appears, as shown in Figure 9-8. You see how many people participated, how many people followed you during the livestream, and how many gifts you received (if any). To dive deeper into your livestream statistics, tap View Analytics.

7. **To exit this screen, tap the X in the upper right.**

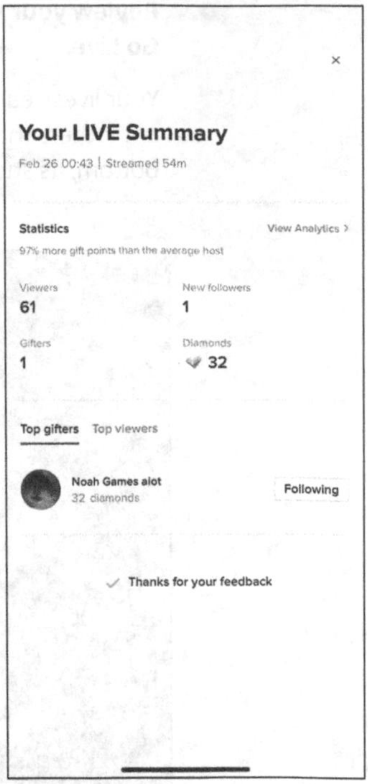

Your LIVE Summary

Feb 26 00:43 | Streamed 54m

Statistics   View Analytics >

9.7% more gift points than the average host

Viewers   New followers
61   1

Gifters   Diamonds
1   32

Top gifters   Top viewers

Noah Games alot   Following
32 diamonds

✓ Thanks for your feedback

FIGURE 9-8:
The live summary page.

There you have it! Stitching, duetting, and going live are just a few of the many things you can do on TikTok as a video creator to reach new audiences, as well as interact more with your existing audience. Take what you've learned here and start thinking of your own creative ways to interact with your audience and others. Before you know it, you might be TikTok famous, too.

Using TikTok as a Business Tool

Chapter **10**

Using TikTok to Grow Your Business

By now, you have been using TikTok regularly and are feeling comfortable with the tools and culture. Maybe you've created a viral video or two, or maybe you just lurk and follow other accounts. Either way, you feel that you've learned enough to want to find out how to get your business on TikTok.

TikTok provides a rich set of tools to show off your company and its products. You can use these tools to provide your business with unique opportunities that could give it an edge against its competitors. That's what this chapter is about!

Understanding How Your Business Fits with TikTok

When consulting or teaching, I always start with the who, what, when, where, and sometimes why regarding what people want to accomplish on social media for their business. In this section, you use the who, what, when, where, and why to figure out whether your business will benefit from TikTok:

>> **Who:** Who do you want to target? It's important to know your target audience and how to fit your business in the TikTok community. I discuss these topics in the next section, "Knowing Your Audience and Competition."

>> **What:** What should you create to engage your audience and meet your business goals? I discuss these issues in "Creating Content That Sells," later in the chapter.

>> **When:** When should you post your business content? To answer this question, you must test, test, and test some more to determine when your audience fulfils your business goals by, for example, buying your products, hiring you for your services, or visiting your website.

TIP

One of my favorite ways to determine when my audience is online most is to click Live (as though I am about to go live, as described in Chapter 9). The page that opens shows how many of my followers are currently online. I then do this throughout the day over a few weeks to determine the times my audience is most likely to see my content.

>> **Where:** Where is it best to post online? Your business and TikTok may not be a good fit. Or maybe having multiple accounts will help you serve the different niches your business serves. I discuss this topic in "Integrating TikTok into Your Funnel."

>> **Why:** Why does your business exist? Why are you trying to use TikTok with your business. How do the answers fit with your mission statement? Are you trying to increase sales or build hype about a product? Do you want to generate traffic to your website?

TIP

You should start with the why, because when you determine that, you can figure out how the who, what, when, and where fit. Discover the why by reviewing or writing down the goals and mission statement for your business.

Knowing Your Audience and Competition

If you reviewed your business's goals and mission statement, you know why you want to use TikTok for your business. Now I want to help you find the who. Here are the steps to get you started:

1. **Segment your audience.**

Look at your list of customers, mailing lists, website and social media demographics, and any other data that will help you understand the audience you want to reach. Then break those demographics down into just three to five demographics. For this exercise, I chose "Customers who like tacos" as one of the demographics for my imaginary taco restaurant.

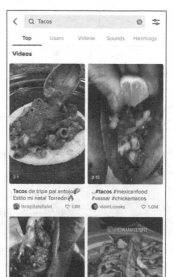

2. **Find each audience demographic on TikTok:**

   a. *Search in TikTok.* Search for common hashtags and topics your audience might talk about. This exercise reveals a list of videos matching that demographic. In Figure 10-1, I looked for an audience interested in tacos.

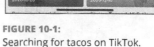

FIGURE 10-1:
Searching for tacos on TikTok.

b. *Use the TikTok ad creation tool.* This powerful approach requires some setup. On a desktop computer, go to `https://ads.tiktok.com` and click Get Started to set up your Ads account (also called a TikTok for Business Account). Follow the onscreen prompts to set up the account, select your ad objectives, and click Continue to start creating an ad.

The ad creation tool displays the approximate number of people in your niche on TikTok. Fill out the demographics on this screen (see Figure 10-2) to see an accurate projection of how many people are in your niche. If this demographic is too small, check out another demographic from those you identified in Step 1. Or maybe TikTok isn't right for your business until more people in that demographic join.

3. **Examine what content works for your target audiences.**

   Using the video search results from Step 2a, determine what types of content works for that audience. Scroll through the top results, tapping on videos that stand out. Create a "Content type" list and note which are most popular.

   The top results for my search were accounts showing their own taco recipes and images of tacos. So for my "Content type" list, I wrote *Recipes* and *Pictures and videos of yummy tacos.*

4. **Look for influencers who might help your brand and niche, sounds that are performing well, and frequently used hashtags.**

Tap the tabs at the top of the search results to see more info:

- *Users:* In the list of users that appears, swipe up to identify users with a lot of followers. Tap your favorites to see if their content represents your audience. Add 10–20 of them to an "Influencers" list, noting how many followers each has, their usernames, and other details you like.

- *Sounds:* A list of top sounds related to your search term appears. Next to each sound is how many times that sound has played. Note sounds with the most plays, add 10–20 of these to a "Top sounds" list, and use them later to choose sounds your audience might already know.

- *Hashtags:* A list of top hashtags related to your search appears, showing the number of views for each hashtag. Make a "Top hashtags" list with the top 10–20 hashtags. As you create content for this demographic, use hashtags from this list in your video descriptions to help TikTok match your content to that audience.

TIP

There are two additional tabs: Videos, which displays a list of videos matching your search criteria, and Top, which is selected by default after your search and displays a list of curated videos, hashtags, sounds, and users. You may find these useful as you search for influencers in your niche.

5. **Repeat Steps 1–4 for your competition's audience.**

If your competition is on TikTok, look at what they're doing, who their audience is, what hashtags work well for their brand, and what sounds they're using. And if you are the first in your niche on TikTok, great — you get to be the pioneer in your niche and your competition has to follow you!

You should now have a comprehensive list of content type, influencers, sounds, and hashtags — both for yourself and your competition. You can now start to figure out where TikTok might fit in your existing marketing efforts, to best reach that audience.

TIP

As you gather information about your audience in the previous steps, keep these tips in mind:

>> **Check out your competition's TikTok profile.** Watch their videos, look for themes in their content, note which videos get the most comments and what the audience is talking about. Check out the hashtags and sounds they use. Which influencers, if any, do they work with? If I had a taco business, I'd consider accounts like @tacobell, @deltaco, and perhaps local restaurants.

>> **If you have fewer than 10,000 followers, choose hashtags with less than a million views.** According to the measurements I see, when users are just starting out, TikTok tends to show content using lesser-viewed hashtags. As your audience grows, choosing higher-viewed hashtags has a greater effect on how often your content is shown to your audience.

>> **Don't choose top-tier influencers with 100,000 or more followers.** They tend to be expensive (as much as $5,000 to $10,000 per post) and have several brands vying for their attention. Instead, choose second- or third-tier influencers who have fewer followers (10,000 to 50,000) but still enough to boost your brand. I'd rather have four or five second-tier influencers who get excited I'm offering them $250 each to post about my brand (some do it for free if you send them product) than a single top influencer who might not care about me or my brand.

SEEKING ADDITIONAL HELP

Feel free to reach out any time to learn more about TikTok-related issues. I consult on social media advertising and strategy for businesses, so I'm happy to help sometimes for free or on a paid basis. Check out this book's Facebook group at https://facebook.com/groups/tiktokfordummies or via the Q&A link on https://tiktok.com/@tiktokfordummiesbook — both are free tools I offer for purchasers of this book. Reach out to me any time at jesse@staynalive.com with your questions or anything you'd like to share.

Integrating TikTok into Your Funnel

A business that uses digital and online channels generally has a path each customer (or audience member or user) travels through — on the company's website and social media platforms — to get to where the business sees results. This path is called a *funnel* because it starts big at the top, with lots of users discovering the product, website, or platform, and gradually shrinks to fewer numbers until a single user *converts* by making a purchase. The idea is to provide content along the funnel to keep users engaged to the point of conversion.

With 60-second (or shorter) videos, TikTok requires a slightly different social media strategy approach than Facebook, Twitter, and YouTube. These tips can guide you when using TikTok in your funnel:

>> **Use TikTok as a gatekeeper to other parts of your funnel.** As short-form content, a quick TikTok video of an employee doing something popular or a duet with another influencer can be a great hook to catch the attention of potential customers. You might embed the video on your website, enticing people to enter their email address to get access to a webinar. Or use the video in a longer video on YouTube or as its own ad on another platform. On TikTok, your video could include a "Click the link in our bio" text in the video or description, enticing users to click to a website landing page that collects more information and takes them further into your funnel for more sales opportunities.

FINDING OUT MORE ABOUT THE FUNNEL

TIP

Russell Brunson (my second cousin) created "The One Funnel Away Challenge," a one-month boot camp about building online funnels. For about $100, you can take the course, which includes books and content mailed to you, along with daily online videos and challenges. I highly recommend it. Sign up at http://bit.ly/OFAforDummies.

Many YouTubers build their YouTube audiences by creating a TikTok video that provides something to engage subscribers and then a call to action in the video to "subscribe to my YouTube channel for more!"

>> **Create direct conversion opportunities with TikTok ads.** Go to `https://ads.tiktok.com` for some great tools that allow you to create TikTok videos that are ads. These videos have links and buttons, which are typically not available in normal TikTok videos, for viewers to click to go to your website or other landing page. Really big advertisers with deep pockets can even do things like take over TikTok with an ad that appears to users when they open the app.

>> **Build buzz.** Word-of-mouth marketing is a great way to get more people into your funnel. Think of what makes a viral video (see Chapter 8) and do what you can to get people talking about your brand organically (without paid ads). Include a link in your bio that takes users to a landing page in your funnel. If your word-of-mouth campaign works, which means users are clicking the link in your bio — boom — they've taken one more step down the sales funnel, and it didn't cost you a thing!

>> **Use your community to promote organic conversion goals.** Remember how I talk about building an audience interested in your niche? The more you focus on building this community by commenting, liking, dueting, stitching, and making them feel important, the more they'll naturally share your content.

Give your community a name, such as TacoTok for my taco restaurant example. Or insert your brand name and address your community as that. For example, a popular meme while I was writing this book was, "show me X without actually showing me X." This meme got the audience thinking creatively and encouraged stitches and engagement. So I could try something like, "Alright, TacoTok, show us your favorite taco from our restaurant, without showing us your favorite taco!"

Creating Content That Sells

I cover the who, where, and why earlier in this chapter. Now I talk about the what. Here are some basic tips for creating business-focused content:

>> **Keep it fun.** Mundane, boring business content you post on other platforms won't cut it here. Using the techniques you've learned elsewhere in this book, your business should create videos that mimic fun ways that regular people in your audience use TikTok. Your videos shouldn't look like ads. Each video you publish should be just another TikTok, with your company acting like any other TikTok user having fun on the platform in creative ways.

TIP

The most popular brands on TikTok use their employees in their videos. One of my favorites is the @washingtonpost account, which features the *Washington Post's* social media guy acting out the most recent popular TikTok memes to tell the news in creative ways. Assign someone similar for your brand to add a creative yet personal touch!

>> **Keep it transparent.** TikTok's community thrives on feeling that everyone is getting a little out of their comfort zone and pulling back the curtain to their life. For your business to succeed, you have to open up and make your followers feel that you, too, are getting out of your comfort zone.

>> **Keep it vertical.** TikTok videos are best recorded in a vertical video format, which is suited for phones. If you try a horizontal (widescreen) format, your video will be harder to see in TikTok and less recognized by the For You page algorithm.

>> **Create brand-focused memes.** If your followers are familiar with your brand and you've built a strong, engaging audience that already comments, duets, and stitches frequently, you can probably convince that audience to try new things. Consider starting new memes, dances, sounds, and trends if you think your audience might respond. Think of creative ways to get your users joining you in your trends, and you may have a viral video take off, without paid ads and with your brand at the center!

>> **Join the conversation.** TikTok is one big community in one big conversation. Know what your followers are talking about and make sure you're part of the conversation. Keep up with popular trends and hashtags to stay relevant — the TikTok community will notice and accept you.

Some rules are made to be broken once in a while. For example, there's a way around the vertical video rule that works well. In your videos, consider breaking the *fourth wall,* which is when an actor or a narrator addresses the audience. One way to do this is based on the fact that audiences view TikTok vertically. In your video, ask your audience to turn their phones horizontally. Then turn the camera horizontally as you're recording, and the audience is watching in full horizontal mode. The video is still in full vertical frame on the viewer's phone, and TikTok will see it as a vertical video, but because the viewers turned their phone sideways it *appears* horizontal to them.

For example, in Figure 10-3, left, I started the video as a vertical video, with a prompt to turn your phone. Then as people turn their phone to the right, the video turns with them, until the entire beautiful Utah landscape from my bedroom balcony appears, as shown in Figure 10-3, right. Go to the video at `https://vm.tiktok.com/ZMeA1BK12/` to see a fun special effect twist.

FIGURE 10-3: The video starts out vertically (left), but as viewers turn their phone, the video ends horizontally.

Chapter **11**

Understanding TikTok Analytics for Your Business

When working with clients, I focus heavily on data to understand how they could see greater success in achieving their goals. Believe it or not, you can measure anything you do on social media — especially on TikTok! In this chapter, I show you how you can analyze just about every element of your TikTok account to meet your business goals.

REMEMBER

The analytics I discuss in this chapter are available only to Business and Creator accounts. Business accounts are suggested for companies or individuals with small businesses and offer three main features: analytics, an email button, and a website link. Creator accounts also offer analytics but are suggested for users and influencers who want to promote themselves as a brand and potentially earn money through their content creation rather than a product. Creator accounts that meet certain requirements are eligible for the Creator Fund and can make money from their videos. If you don't see either option on the Settings and Privacy page, tap Manage Account, and then tap Switch to Business Account. Answer the onscreen questions, and you'll be set up in a matter of minutes.

Knowing Which Data Is Important

The first question I ask my social media clients is, "How are you currently tracking your social media?" I review every tool they use, so that I can discover how to extract data from each one. As you use TikTok, you should understand the data available to you as well.

I recommend that you track the following parts of TikTok. Unless specified, TikTok Analytics, covered in the next section, gives you at least minimal data for each of these. You might want to look into other analytics platforms (a few are listed in the final section of this chapter) for additional measurements of each of these elements listed:

>> **Top videos:** Look at the views for each video and the combined views for all your videos. The more views you have, the more your videos will show up on the For You page! Also examine which videos have the most comments, likes, duets, and stitches and what you did in each video, so you can understand the type of content that works best for your account.

>> **Followers:** Track your number of followers and follower growth over time. If follower growth is slowing, reevaluate the focus of your videos.

>> **Follower demographics:** The more you know about your followers, the better you can create content that matches their interests.

>> **Follower activity times:** Knowing when followers are active will show you the best times to post.

>> **Conversions:** You should track how your videos are accomplishing your business goals so you can know how your videos affect your bottom line.

Understanding TikTok Analytics

TikTok provides an analytics tool to help you track many parts of TikTok beyond the number of followers and video views. You access these analytics by tapping the three dots in the upper-right corner of your profile page and then tapping either Creator Tools or Business Suite on the Settings and Profile page. From there, tap Analytics, and you're in.

The TikTok Analytics screen has four tabs at the top that display data for your account:

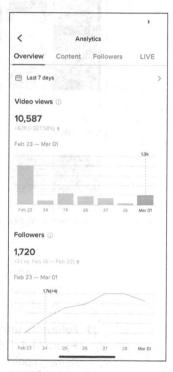

FIGURE 11-1:
The analytics overview screen.

» **Overview:** Tap the Overview tab, shown in Figure 11-1, to see the following snapshot of your entire account:

- *Video Views:* The total views for all your videos in the last seven days, the growth from the previous seven days, and a day-by-day bar graph of total video views

- *Followers:* The total followers for your account in the last seven days, the growth from the previous seven days, and a day-by-day line graph of total new followers

- *Profile Views:* The number of times your profile was viewed in the last seven days, the growth from the previous seven days, and a day-by-day bar graph of profile views

» **Content:** Tap the Content tab to display the content screen, shown in Figure 11-2. This screen displays the following data about your content:

- *Video Posts:* The number of posts over the last seven days, and a list of each video, showing total views for that video. Tap the video to see more (see Figure 11-3).

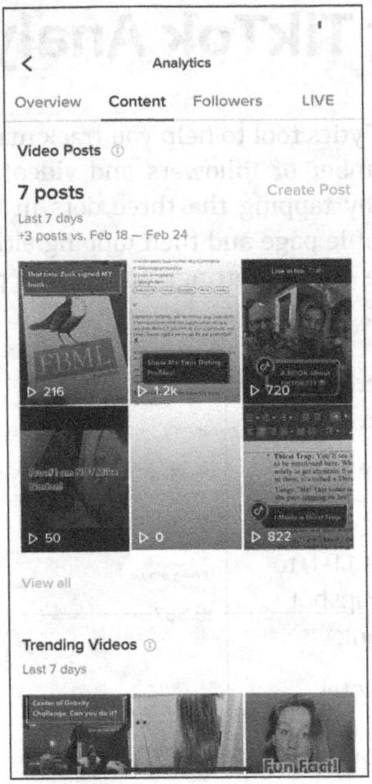

FIGURE 11-2:
The content analytics screen.

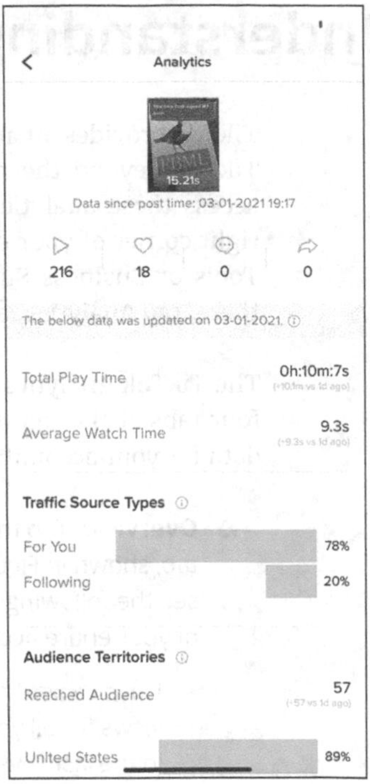

FIGURE 11-3:
Individual video analytics.

- *Trending Videos.* A list of videos with more new views than others in the past seven days. Tap each one to see its individual video analytics.

» **Followers tab:** Tap to display the followers screen, shown in Figure 11-4. This screen displays data about your followers' demographics:

  - *Followers:* The number of followers for your account. If you have fewer than 100 followers, this is the only metric you'll see in this tab.

  - *Gender:* The percentage of male to female followers.

  - *Top Territories:* The top countries and areas of the world where your followers live.

TIP

Use follower demographic data to determine what types of content will resonate most with your existing audience.

- *Follower Activity:* Swipe down to the bottom of the screen to see what times your followers are most active. Tap Days on the right to see on which days your followers are most active.

TIP

Take note of follower activity data. Then experiment to find out whether you see more views and achieve other business goals by posting during more popular times.

» **Live:** The Live tab appears if you have more than 1,000 followers. The Live screen, shown in Figure 11-5, provides the following stats for your livestreams:

- *Basic stats:* The top section shows the number of live videos you performed in the last 7 or 28 days, the number of views on those videos combined, the number of new followers you gained from your livestreams, the time viewers spent on all livestreams, and the top viewer count (maximum number of viewers watching a single video at a time) across all livestreams. Tap the *X* Live Videos text to dive deeper into analytics for each individual livestream.

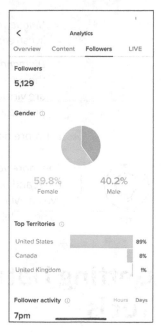

FIGURE 11-4:
Checking demographic data.

FIGURE 11-5:
The live analytics category.

- *Unique viewers:* The number of unique viewers of your livestreams over the past 7 or 28 days.

- *Diamonds:* The number of diamonds you received over the past 7 or 28 days across all livestreams. *Diamonds* are virtual gifts that users 18 years and older can purchase, send, or receive.

For more on livestreaming, see Chapter 9.

TIP

The more you go live, the more opportunities you have to meet and build relationships with new followers. Use the live analytics to help you use your livestreams as effectively as possible!

Getting Data from Third-Party Tools

Although TikTok has several great analytics tools of its own, as described in this chapter and Chapter 7, I also use the following third-party analytics platforms regularly:

>> **StatisTok:** This tool studies everything it can about your TikTok account and uses statistical data to identify the best times to post, top hashtags on your account, top sounds on your account, and more. Visit http://bit.ly/ttfdstatistok and use code jessestay at signup for a 10-day free trial of their Pro subscription, which they're offering just to readers of this book!

>> **TOK Board:** This tool indexes the top sounds of the week and month so you can identify new and trending songs for your videos. It displays by how much each song has grown in popularity in the past week, letting you know if the song is about to go viral. Go to https://tokboard.com/.

The Part of Tens

Discover ten of my favorite TikTok accounts that I think you should follow.

Get my ten best tips for building followers on TikTok.

Look at ten brands that are doing it right on TikTok.

Chapter **12**

My Ten Favorite TikTok Accounts

A s I've studied TikTok the past few years, several accounts have stood out. They always make me smile or teach me something. To me, the ten accounts listed in this chapter summarize the essence of what makes TikTok, well, tick!

Learning about ADHD with Catieosaurus

Catie O, or Catieosaurus as she prefers to be called (see Figure 12-1), provides an entertaining and safe space to learn about the challenges of ADHD from someone with ADHD (like myself). Be prepared to laugh and join her #fruitsnack-nation of fruit snack lovers waiting for her next video! Follow her at https://tiktok.com/@catieosaurus.

Courtesy of Catie O (@catieosaurus)

FIGURE 12-1: @catieosaurus offers fruit snacks for a sensitive ADHD topic.

Drawing with Dan Povenmire

You might recognize Dan Povenmire when you hear him duet with other TikTokers as "Dr. Doofenschmirtz," the evil professor from the Disney cartoon, *Phineas and Ferb.* Dan is co-creator of the cartoon and does an amazing job interacting with his followers and fans, bringing a level of transparency to his personal life. Follow Dan at https://tiktok.com/@danpovenmire.

Following the Journey with Lexi McDonald

Lexi McDonald, shown connecting with her community in Figure 12-2, uses her account to share her personal journey of leaving the religion she grew up in. She respectfully discusses the effect it has had on her loved ones, and the difficulties and life changes she has made while transitioning away from everything she has known. By sharing her journey, she joined thousands of others with similar experiences, all helping each other realize they're not alone.

I love Lexi's account because it showcases the point that no one is alone on TikTok. Try it with your own challenges and see! Follow Lexi at https://tiktok.com/@exmolex.

Courtesy of Lexi McDonald (@exmolex)

FIGURE 12-2:
Lexi McDonald shares raw truths about her faith journey.

Dancing with Bao Tran

In this entertaining account, dancer Bao Tran teaches you how to do viral TikTok dances. He even provides slow-motion videos you can easily follow and then play at double or triple speed to look like you danced in real time! Check him out at https://tiktok.com/@learnhowtodance0.

Interacting with Cheech & Chong

Readers of my generation and older will be familiar with the ever-loving comedian stoners Cheech & Chong. To continue working together while social distancing during Covid-19, they launched a TikTok account in which they interact in a laid-back and humorous way, as you can see in Figure 12-3. They now have 2 million fans! The duo spends their days interacting, dueting, and stitching with other followers on TikTok. (*Note:* Younger kids may want to stay away from this one or have an adult around.)

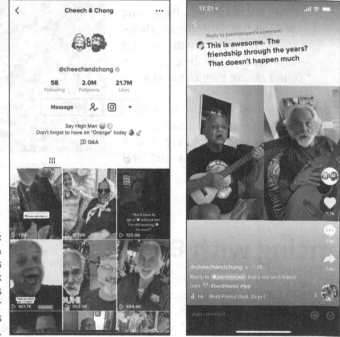

FIGURE 12-3: Cheech & Chong's TikTok account is full of their interactions with fans.

Cheech & Chong are a great example of using TikTok to introduce fans to your life, revealing the real you no matter how famous you are. Everyone is equal on TikTok! Follow them at https://tiktok.com/@cheechandchong.

Making Money with Trevin Peterson

Trevin Peterson caught my attention with videos that show his followers how they can make money on TikTok through Amazon's FBA platform (see Figure 12-4). Trevin uses his large TikTok audience to drive traffic and views to his YouTube channel and other funnels where he teaches people how to sell on Amazon. Trevin's content is a great example of using TikTok as a component in your existing business funnel, as I discuss in Chapter 10. Follow Trevin at https://tiktok.com/@trevin peterson.

Courtesy of Trevin Peterson (@trevinpeterson)

FIGURE 12-4:
Trevin Peterson showcases his Amazon inventory.

Sharing Pride with Josh Helfgott

Josh Helfgott is a TikToker and activist who uses his platform to promote equality and upbeat stories about the LGBTQ community. Josh represents the type of attitude TikTok wants its users to embrace. He brings a positive message while driving awareness to a topic that some, unfortunately, find offensive. As an ally to the LGBTQ community, I learn something from all his videos. Follow Josh at https://tiktok.com/@joshhelfgott.

Getting Inspired with Shontez Davis

I asked TikTokers to share their story for inclusion in the book, and Shontez commented. I immediately fell in love with his content and his story. Shontez has only one leg, and he talks about his life, including his weight-loss journey and the challenges he has faced. Shontez shows a sense of humor in all his videos, making his story and journey not only interesting but entertaining. I'm glad he found my account and offered his story! Follow Shontez at `https://tiktok.com/@onelegwonderr`.

Anchoring the News with Marcus DiPaola

Marcus DiPaola is a former White House press corps reporter who has turned his career entirely to TikTok to anchor the news in "a writing style designed to make it possible for middle schoolers with learning disabilities to understand the news" (according to his website at `https://marcusdipaola.medium.com/hi-7a1fe48050f1`). Marcus's TikTok account is straightforward and easy to understand, and it sticks to real journalism and unbiased reporting in one-minute (or shorter) segments. He reported live from the violent scene at the Capitol during the 2021 Capitol riot.

I think TikTok is changing the landscape of news and content consumption, like Twitter did in its early days, and Markus is a good example of that change. You can follow Marcus at `https://tiktok.com/@marcus.dipaola`.

Learning about TikTok Trends with Jera Bean

While I plan to show off as many trends as I can on the @tiktokfordummiesbook account for this book, one account does an even more exceptional job, at least at the time of this writing (hey — I'm always up for a challenge!). Jera Bean has built an impressive list of the latest TikTok trends and shows you in step-by-step detail how to re-create each.

Jera also demonstrates the trends, as well as tips and tricks for growing a large following on TikTok and getting views on your videos. As a fellow TikTok marketing geek, Jera speaks my language. Check out Jera at https://tiktok.com/@jera.bean.

Chapter **13**

Ten TikTok Business Accounts Doing It Right

TikTok's mantra for businesses is, "Don't create ads. Create TikToks!" It's clear that TikTok wants businesses to use TikTok the same way most other people use the service: by putting humans in front. Having led social media strategy for large enterprise environments, smaller local business clients, and well-known charities, I endorse this approach for brands using any social network. In this chapter, I highlight business accounts on TikTok that emulate this "TikToks over ads" approach to drive income.

TIP

I want to try a little brand experiment. As you visit each account listed in this chapter, find your favorite video on that brand's account, and comment with "@tiktokfordummiesbook sent me!" or similar. Let's see if we can do some influencing of our own. Perhaps someday at least one of these accounts will include this book in one of their videos!

Sharing the News with *The Washington Post*

The Washington Post uses TikTok the way most brands should use TikTok. If your business is using TikTok, I recommend that you assign an employee or two to manage your business account and let them use TikTok as your brand, the way any other TikTok user would use TikTok. Just make sure your business monitors this account and maintains some sort of contractual agreement on what happens to the TikTok account when the employee leaves. *The Washington Post* shows how this should be done, perfectly, at www.tiktok.com/@washingtonpost.

FIGURE 13-1:
@washingtonpost assigns a reporter to be the main actor of their TikTok account.

They assigned one reporter, Dave Jorgenson, to their TikTok account, and he reports on and acts out the news. See Figure 13-1. Dave presents the news in entertaining and fun ways, following TikTok trends, topics, and memes. I've seen Dave dance popular TikTok dances, lip sync popular sounds on TikTok, and act out fun skits to tell the day's news. *The Washington Post's* TikTok account has made consuming the news fun for me.

Knowing Your Audience with Taco Bell

Taco Bell is one of my favorite brands on TikTok not only because I love tacos and am a frequent visitor but also because they do an exceptional job of understanding their audience — Gen Z, the current teenagers and young adults of the world. The account features young-looking actors and influencers who speak well to that audience, all eating their favorite taco products from Taco Bell.

The account does a good job embracing the latest trends, from spinning drinks using the popular time warp waterfall effect (see Figure 13-2, right) to typing messages in real-time using the typing effect (see Figure 13-2, left). The account is even known to allow cursing in a humorous way, bleeped out with the Taco Bell bell sound. You can follow Taco Bell at www.tiktok.com/@tacobell.

FIGURE 13-2: @tacobell using the time warp waterfall effect (right), and an actor for the account typing in real-time about a new product (left).

Partnering with Dunkin'

I became familiar with Dunkin's TikTok account because several popular influencers drink their coffee and conveniently include it in their videos. And if you shop at Dunkin' for their coffee, you might be familiar with their popular drink, the Charli, shown in Figure 13-3, designed in partnership with Dunkin' by one of TikTok's most followed users, Charli Damelio (@charlidamelio), who has more than 110 million followers.

Dunkin' does a masterful job recruiting and partnering with influences big and small, getting those influencers to use Dunkin' products in their videos. Dunkin' uses TikTok the way a typical user does: They respond and engage with their followers both large and small and are known to interact with TikTok users

FIGURE 13-3:
@dunkin's the Charli.

and even feature their videos that include Dunkin' products.

I'm betting Dunkin' has an entire team or digital marketing agency devoted to identifying when @dunkin is mentioned, reviewing videos containing Dunkin' products, and deciding what videos to respond to, what to feature on the @dunkin account, and who needs a product named after them. I'm in awe of the complexity of their approach and look forward to the day when I, too, can have a coffee named after me or this book. You can follow Dunkin' at www.tiktok.com/@dunkin.

Dancing with Break the Floor

Break the Floor, at www.tiktok.com/@breakthefloor, is a dance company that uses TikTok well. They partner, just like Dunkin', with one of TikTok's most popular users, Charli Damelio (@charlidamelio), who is known for starting several of the original dance trends on TikTok. This smaller-sized company can now recruit top-tier dancers due to the attention they garner on TikTok.

Break the Floor does a great job finding and sharing trends showcasing the talent of its dancers. For instance, one video on their account shows the poise of a ballerina staying completely still while duetting others using the time warp scan effect, as shown in Figure 13-4.

FIGURE 13-4:
@breakthefloor featuring the finesse of a ballerina by using a popular effect.

Break the Floor represents the type of brand that utilizes people with significant artistic or performing talent. By tapping into this talent, they can produce creative and interesting content to keep their followers and potential new students and audiences wanting to see more.

Placing Product with Pop Sockets

Pop Sockets, a small product for holding your phone, is everywhere on TikTok. The company is doing a great job placing their product in the hands of as many influencers as they can.

The Pop Sockets TikTok account (www.tiktok.com/@popsockets) includes fun trends that any user can try. They have partnered with popular influencers to showcase their own Pop Sockets on their phones while recording Q&As about each influencer in a mirror, as shown in Figure 13-5, poking fun at a way many users like to record their videos.

On top of influencer partnerships and the organic use and creation of trends, Pop Sockets has also sponsored several ad campaigns on TikTok to promote trends and to get people using several #popsocket themed hashtags.

FIGURE 13-5:
@popsockets featuring a Q&A in a mirror, reflecting their product.

Playing Sports with the Utah Jazz Bear

Living in Utah, I'm a fan of the Utah Jazz (as well as the Houston Rockets, from my years growing up in Houston). The Utah Jazz Bear account is so entertaining! The popular NBA basketball team, the Utah Jazz, uses this account to feature none other than its own team mascot, the Utah Jazz Bear.

On the Utah Jazz Bear account, at www.tiktok.com/@utahjazz bear, every video features the Utah Jazz Bear performing gymnastic stunts, throwing himself through basketball hoops, embracing TikTok trends, and more. He does all this fully suited up and not saying a word. As you can see in Figure 13-6, the Utah

Jazz Bear also likes to perform popular TikTok dances, recruiting the team's cheerleaders and Utah Jazz Dancers to further promote entertainment you might see at a Utah Jazz basketball game. He even promotes team spirit by competing, in duets, with other competing NBA team mascots.

The Utah Jazz Bear is an excellent example of utilizing every asset you have as a brand to provide a creative and entertaining experience for your audience. In this case, the Utah Jazz embraced an employee already good at acting and entertaining in costume, gave that person a TikTok account, and said, "Go wild!"

FIGURE 13-6: @utahjazzbear performing a TikTok dance with a Utah Jazz Dancer.

Recruiting Influencers with Bang Energy

As a dad of teenagers, I'm all too familiar with the Bang Energy brand. What would a teenager or young adult be these days without an energy drink in their hands? Bang Energy has a product that most of the Gen Z audience on TikTok is already familiar with. Like many of the other brands listed here, they've found creative ways to get free product to influencers, ensuring that the Bang Energy drink brand is shared far and wide, both on and off the Bang Energy TikTok account.

On the Bang Energy account itself, at www.tiktok.com/ @bangenergy, the company incorporates themes users would typically see surfing through their For You pages. They hire dancers to perform fun dances their audience can try, making sure the video's colors match their new drinks, which are displayed up front, as shown in Figure 13-7. The account also includes influencers such as @ironsanctuary doing things they are known for doing on their own accounts, but with the Bang Energy drink prominently placed in the video.

They created a separate @bangenergy.ceo account for the CEO of the company, whom they mention frequently in their videos. When the CEO doesn't have much time to do a lot of TikToks, they populate the account with additional TikTok-familiar content featuring the drink in creative ways, with an occasional video from the CEO himself. This use of the CEO with his own account makes the business feel a bit more personal to the company's followers.

FIGURE 13-7:
Bang brings in dancers to create a dance for their latest energy drink.

Entertaining with *The Tonight Show* Starring Jimmy Fallon

If you follow my personal account, @jessestay, you'll know that I have a warped sense of humor and love comedy. I think that *The Tonight Show* Starring Jimmy Fallon is the gold standard for comedy, and that Jimmy Fallon can't go wrong with his account, @fallontonight.

The *Tonight Show* account partners with guests on the show to make creative, usually funny videos alongside host Jimmy Fallon and his band, the Roots. You will laugh as you surf from video to video, seeing Fallon act out the latest trends with popular movie and TV stars, such as a parody with popular singer John Legend of a year of quarantine during the pandemic. The show's account even features @jimmyfallon performing a skit remotely with another celebrity on TikTok, while in lockdown during the Covid-19 pandemic, as shown in Figure 13-8.

FIGURE 13-8: @fallontonight featuring Jimmy Fallon doing a skit remotely with another celebrity.

TikTok is a new entertainment medium for today's short-attention-span youth. *The Tonight Show* Starring Jimmy Fallon has recognized that superbly and taken their vast content library of skits performed live on the show and put them in short (60 seconds or less), entertaining, vertical videos. By doing so, they give the show a new medium for entertaining a younger generation. They then use this format to promote other formats that older generations may already be familiar with for additional ad revenue.

The Tonight Show brand is an amazing example of how a business in the video entertainment industry can adapt to younger audiences by understanding their interests. You can follow *The Tonight Show* Starring Jimmy Fallon at www.tiktok.com/@ fallontonight.

Being Prepared with the American Red Cross

Having spent some time working with nonprofits, I would be remiss to not include a good example of nonprofits using TikTok. The American Red Cross is one of my favorites. As an eagle scout and former scoutmaster in the Boy Scouts, and coming out of a global pandemic, being prepared for any situation is a priority. With @americanredcross in my feed, I receive reminders on how to do just that.

The American Red Cross has given their account to one of their younger employees who serves as the actor in each video. She acts out emergency situations, vaccine effectiveness (see Figure 13-9, left), the Heimlich maneuver, and other safety protocols, while narrating how to perform each in a way that's easy for younger viewers to understand.

FIGURE 13-9: @americanredcross shows the effectiveness of vaccines (left) and features a donate button for their own charity (right).

The account includes videos showcasing what other volunteers are doing around the US for the nonprofit and shows how you can volunteer as well. Other videos show you how to donate and how to add Red Cross charity buttons to your profile (see Figure 13-9, right), so visitors can donate right in TikTok.

The relatability of this account to a younger audience interested in doing something good for the world is why I featured this amazing nonprofit. Be sure to follow the American Red Cross at www.tiktok.com/@americanredcross for more great examples for your nonprofit.

Engaging Your Audience with Chipotle

Chipotle, the well-known restaurant known for its burritos, is all over TikTok. I first discovered the @chipotle account when they sponsored a hashtag-based TikTok advertisement that appeared when I opened the TikTok app. It was an ad partnering with popular influencer David Dobrik (@daviddobrik), who is known for giving away extravagant items to his followers on social media, asking why people should win $10,000 from Chipotle and David Dobrik himself. Soon TikTok was filled with videos of duets and stitches with people competing for the $10,000, all promoting Chipotle.

The Chipotle brand is a master at getting people talking about its burritos, with similar challenges and cross-promotional ad campaigns that get TikTok talking. They even did a promotion offering to name a burrito after one lucky person who submitted the best burrito recipe.

I like Chipotle's use of TikTok so much I've even incorporated some of the Chipotle strategy into the promotion of this book. Shortly before this book went to print, I offered to let anyone who duets their favorite TikTok feature to have their account featured in the acknowledgments of this book, as shown in Figure 13-10. Dozens of people talked about the book, all excited to be featured. You may be one of those reading this now. Well, skip a few more pages to the acknowledgments, and you can see how successful that campaign was, inspired by Chipotle's TikTok account. You can follow Chipotle at www.tiktok.com/@chipotle.

Now I want a burrito and some coffee. If you do, too, and have been checking out each of the accounts in this chapter as I have, I hope you can see how effective brands using TikTok are!

FIGURE 13-10:
I'm on @tiktokfordummiesbook, taking inspiration from Chipotle for a duet campaign.

Chapter **14**

Ten Ways to Grow Your Following

n Chapters 7, 8, and 10, I share some strategies for growing an audience on TikTok. Here I share my top ten tips that can help you attract more followers. Implement these tips and watch your numbers skyrocket.

Be Transparent and Vulnerable

TikTok is built to make you a little uncomfortable. I'm a writer. I hate standing in front of a camera and seeing myself on film doing weird and awkward things. But that's the point of TikTok! If you get past being uncomfortable, you'll realize that everyone on TikTok is doing the same thing.

Due to the network's informal, quick video format, most people get away with no makeup and poor lighting. Some people are still in their pajamas! But they are having fun with their new community. The more you open up your life and find your own story, the more you'll find your community on TikTok. Your followers will naturally grow in that process. On TikTok, you don't fit in when you're *not* transparent!

Stay Consistent

Consistency is key on TikTok. Find your niche and stick to it. Part of being transparent is discovering what stories you have to tell the world. Figure that out, and make sure every one of your videos focuses on that story. Soon, your audience will come to expect that story and want more. Then others will become part of your story. And the TikTok algorithm will know much better which audiences will be most likely to follow your content when it appears on their For You page.

Know Your Audience

After you have a story, start thinking about who might want to hear that story. As you stay consistent in your story, it's important to address a consistent audience as well. Your audience might prefer to hear certain things and be offended by others. Some topics will prompt them to comment more than others. Research your audience using the tips in Chapter 11, and make sure your content is always created for this audience. As you do this, new followers will find you as TikTok selects your content as the type of content they're most likely to follow.

Include Your Community

After you identify your audience, you'll notice an interesting phenomenon. They'll make videos together, dueting, stitching, and communicating around your target niche. (You're consistent in that niche, right?) A community forms and grows, with you at the helm, bringing more and more followers to your account.

Build Up and Promote Others

In Chapter 5, I suggest that you read *How to Win Friends and Influence People.* The secret to having any form of influence, especially on TikTok, is to genuinely build up others around you. Find ways to use your account to promote other TikTokers and then share their success. See someone in need in your audience or community? Find a way to help.

Engage Your Audience

I mention in Chapter 5 that the single best thing you can do to grow followers and increase video views is to get your audience to engage with your content. Most importantly, get them to comment on your videos. Then see if you can get them to duet or stitch your videos. The more they do this, the more their followers and similar users will see your content on their For You pages.

Be Entertaining

Being entertaining isn't easy, but you can be entertaining in different ways. Sometimes simply sharing a unique story is entertaining. In addition, TikTok provides tools you can use to add entertaining elements to your videos. Add an effect that turns you into a unicorn. Dance to a song. Lip sync to your favorite artist or to a funny TV or comedy sketch. In each video, try to add something to catch and hold your audience's attention.

REMEMBER

The TikTok algorithm rewards videos that maintain the viewer's attention the longest. I recommend that the first thing you do in your video is catch the viewer's attention. Try something funny or controversial, or even say something like, "Wait until the end to see. . . ." This is the first step to entertaining your viewers and keeping their attention to the very end.

Join Other Influencers

Every time I duet or stitch a video with a popular influencer or a viral video, I see more video views than usual, and often more followers if I've given people a reason to follow me. Pay attention to trends and join them when you can, and you should notice the same. For example, I noticed a viral video of two girls randomly laughing. Soon other TikTokers were dueting with them, while the girls laughed at whatever was said. I tried it, and the girls laughed while I shared the idea that I was writing a book about TikTok. By having them laugh as a duet at my expense, I saw a tenfold increase on that video.

Follow Similar Accounts

Identify and follow three to five popular accounts on TikTok with followers you want to attract. Users who aren't already popular will often follow you back. Follow the real and engaging followers of those three to five accounts, and you can strategically increase followers in your niche as they, in turn, follow you back.

TIP

If you want to automate the process of following people who are following other accounts in your niche, use a tool such as FuelTok (`http://bit.ly/ttfdfueltok`), which can automatically identify and follow accounts that are likely to follow you back. Just make sure whatever tool you use is following *only* the accounts you want it to — FuelTok is one I trust.

Another follower-generation tool I recommend that currently works only with Instagram followers is Flock (`http://bit.ly/ttfdflocksocial`). Keep watching Flock, because they are popular and I bet they'll support TikTok soon.

WARNING

Many services have created millions of fake accounts and will charge $1,000 or so to guarantee lots of followers. What you get is nothing but fake accounts that don't engage or buy anything. Be cautious in this space!

Go Live

Every time you go live, TikTok encourages people to join your livestream, potentially gaining new followers for your account. If you're eligible to use this feature (you need 1,000+ followers), try to go live as often as you can to interact with your community and attract more followers.

Index

G

Gender metric, 162
gestures, 2
GIF Maker app, 133
giving, influencers and, 94
going live, 190
gossip, 121
graphic content, 96
Green Screen category, 52
growing your following, 187–190

H

Hanania, Aaron (TikTok user), 129
harassment, 96
hashtags, 80–81, 121
Heart icon, 27
Helfgott, Josh, 171
Home screen, browsing on, 25–27
horizontal orientation, 158
How to Win Friends and Influence People (Carnegie), 92, 189

I

icons
Comment (word balloon), 27
Direct Messages (DMs), 33
Duet, 138
Effects, 144
Enhance, 143
explained, 3
Flip, 43, 143
Heart, 27
Not Interested, 30
+, 42
Remember, 3
Settings, 144
Share, 27, 144
Speed, 43
Technical Stuff, 3
Tip, 3
Video creator's profile pic, 27
Warning, 3
identifying trending content, 124–128
illegal activities, 96
iMovie app, 133
inbox notifications, 33–37
influencers
about, 92–94
joining, 190
Instagram, featuring in profile, 15
integrity, 97
Interactive category, 52
Internet resources
American Red Cross, 185
Bang Energy, 181
Bean, Jera, 173
Break the Floor, 179
Catieosaurus, 168
Cheat Sheet, 3
Cheech & Chong, 170
Chipotle, 186
Davis, Shontez, 172
DiPaola, Marcus, 172
Dunkin' Donuts, 178
Flock, 190
FuelTok, 190
Helfgott, Josh, 171
McDonald, Lexi, 169
"The One Funnel Away Challenge," 155
Peterson, Trevin, 171
Pop Sockets, 180
Povenmire, Dan, 168
StatisTok, 164
Taco Bell, 177
TOK Board, 164
The Tonight Show Starring Jimmy Fallon, 183
Tran, Bao, 169
Utah Jazz Bear, 180
The Washington Post, 176
invoking emotion, 131

J

joining influencers, 190
Jorgenson, Dave (reporter), 176

K

'Karen,' 89
Kindle Fire devices, 10
knowing your audience/ competition, 151–154, 188

L

Landscape filter, 54
launching
Discover page, 124
For You page (FYP), 26
Lee, Elisha (TikTok influencer), 132
length
of clips, 64
of videos, 43, 122–123
like feature, 27–30, 90–91
Likes metric, 114, 116
live, going, 190

About the Author

Jesse Stay is an author of ten books including one of the first published books on Facebook, the first book on Facebook application development, and now with this book, one of the first published books on TikTok. Jesse is an accomplished and world-renowned speaker and an all-around expert in technology, especially in the areas of social media and social media marketing. (Facebook and Myspace are former clients of his!) Jesse eats, breaths, and sleeps TikTok, Facebook, Twitter, and other future-leaning and connecting technologies. Most recently, Jesse wrote *Minecraft For Dummies* and *Minecraft Recipes For Dummies* with two of his sons, Thomas and Joseph.

Jesse's mission in life is to bring balance to the personal, work, and family life of others. He does this using his talents to teach others how to automate their lives with world-changing technology. A computer programmer since he was 9, Jesse understands what it's like to find an immersive piece of software that has the potential to connect the world in new ways. Not since Facebook has he seen a connected environment like TikTok!

In his spare time, you can find Jesse hanging out as a single dad with his seven kids whenever they'll give him time. His most recent passions as a newly single dad (outside TikTok, of course) are understanding the data behind dating apps, relationship psychology, and dynamics, and teaching other men how to become better men from his studies. He's also a bit of a bitcoin and cryptocurrency nerd!

If any of these things pique your interest, you can find Jesse through his own website at http://jessestay.com and follow him on TikTok at http://tiktok.com/@jessestay!

Dedication

To my forever-friends, Ellie, Reese, and Joni, who influenced me to try TikTok. You're always alright, by me!

Author's Acknowledgments

Thanks to everyone who had patience with me as I put things aside in the middle of a global pandemic to focus on finishing this book. To my kids at home — Joseph, JJ, Alex, Emily, and Juliet (who was the subject of my first 1 million+ view TikTok video!) — thanks especially for dealing with Dad being up late and in his office focused on this book, unable to give you as much time as I should. Thanks to my son Thomas, away on a religious mission as I wrote this, for reading my emails about the book remotely. And to my son Louis: I say this with tears in my eyes, thank you for being you!

As always, thanks to all the staff at Wiley and all those who worked with me on this book. Thanks especially to my copy editor, Susan Pink, for having patience with my crazy schedule and pushing me stay on task; Nicole, who "dummified" a lot of my content and helped keep the book on schedule; Hannah Partridge, my tech editor; Steve Hayes, who allowed this crazy TikTok book dream to become reality; and my book agent, Carole Jelen, for helping me present this idea to Wiley. I couldn't have written this without any of you.

And lastly, thanks to all who participated, right on TikTok, in the making of this book! All of the following TikTok handles had a major part in building the *TikTok For Dummies* community (follow it using the #tiktokfordummies hashtag) — you should go follow them!

@seperatecanada
@nonbinarygeekyparent
@iamahufflepuffandproud
@eggysplat
@jessepyrotv
@mythical_banana1
@xpierced_tfgx
@buddyzee_fisher
@elairianlync
@jeremysnotfunny
@grayhairwhere
@dashawnjtharpine
@living_the_shunt_life
@brinksenc

@therealtimothyweber
@aaronhanania
@drstoooopid
@edwardthomas7
@way2fiesty4u1
@michelle85tt1
@buddyzee_fisher
@trans_but_great_hair
@claystewart54
@daniellecasperhar
@papi_krabs
@darkweebau
@jjstarr2005
@herotomillions

@owen__kushner
@captainrexx66
@killedformama
@ongakupunk
@fbi___2.0
@thrsimplordr6
@f22boi
@mr_ghost_man
@mrcyph3rr
@shatugi_sama
@itrytocookandfail
@littleprinncessfox
@prayforpeace16
@split_mango
@rex88809
@animalcrossingaddictions
@thisonegood1
@darthdoggo666
@_andy_rew_fish
@jokerandbats0
@gamersocaiety
@2018_audi_s5_official
@spyguysgaming
@sairrry
@nolanweber14
@levi_hughes3
@definitely_not_ethan95
@kylorenstiktok
@smoney_93
@nightmint08
@og_soan
@foxclan43
@dpgjack
@s.t.o.n.k.s
@samsonlovesoggywaffles
@bradyslrr
@yes_a_ama_bannana_slug
@creepysingz
@killer.nightmare_
@stuff_and_things
@urasissie
@darthdylan_
@herothefur
@highlandtnt303
@_tj_tj_2007_
@runningwaterfromthetap
@the2ndimposter1
@char.com.co
@wellimhereandlikebasebal
@freedyofficial1
@black_playstationcontrol
@hamstagang32
@spicy_wat3r
@ashtonantrim
@moose_gaming_
@perisankianrouchi
@shaneyb1122
@djtyedupofficial
@zachgreen31
@trump2024694201
@brosephgaming
@mr.broverse2
@gamerguythayne
@princesslunaz
@technolotl
@snowlife000
@holdupbouttapog
@l_.m00nlight._l
@extreemrcs
@fishstick_and_llama
@h00d_e_dj
@erentard42069
@deathisuponus12
@destoryergray17
@galaxycell099
@lucidnightmare
@thegreatturtlemaster
@ynwaustinx
@hogdude
@amyfrantaa

Publisher's Acknowledgments

Executive Editor: Steve Hayes

Project Editor: Susan Pink

Copy Editor: Susan Pink

Technical Editor: Hannah Partridge

Proofreader: Debbye Butler

Production Editor: Tamilmani Varadharaj

Cover Image: © WAYHOME studio, © Jun Takahashi/Photodisc/ Getty Images